Published by Galore Park Publishing Ltd.,
PO Box 96, Cranbrook, Kent TN17 4WS
www.galorepark.co.uk

Translation copyright ©Betty Halifax 2003

Design copyright ©Galore Park Publishing Ltd 2003

Designed by Brian Pearce

Printed by Ashford Colour Press Ltd, Unit 600, Fareham
Reach, Fareham Road, Gosport, Hants PO13 OFW

ISBN 1 902984 24 2

With grateful thanks to Roger Dalladay for supplying
the pictures used in this book, and to Brian Pearce for
the design.

First Published 2003

Front cover: Mummy portrait from Roman Egypt (British Museum)

# A TASTE
## OF
# LATIN POETRY

### Translated by
# BETTY HALIFAX

GALORE PARK

ho do you want to go to as a present, little book?

Quick! Find a guardian, little waif,

Somebody who'll keep you safe,

Not some predatory rotter

Who'll whisk you into his kitchen clutter

And use you as a makeshift dish,

Make you soggy with fried fish,

Or twist you round until he's got

A cone-shaped paper pepper pot.


MARTIAL


*A 25 page selection from these translations was awarded a Special Commendation by the British Comparative Literature Association.*

# INTRODUCTION

This book is intended for any readers who are interested in poetry, whether they have read the original Latin or not, and who enjoy literature which has influenced European civilisation and often provided a model for later writers. The poems range from the tender to the bawdy, from domestic trivia to philosophy. In fact the aim has been to provide a complete picture of Roman life and to show that the Romans did not spend all their time tramping with the legions and conquering Gaul. The art of translating, especially poetry, is a difficult one: the vocabulary and spirit of the original must be preserved, yet the finished product must be acceptable in the new tongue. In the hope of achieving the necessary balance, I have tried to keep as close as possible to the Latin but have made occasional modifications, especially with names, to help elucidate points which otherwise might be obscure. I have also attempted to keep the spirit of the Latin authors by imposing some discipline of form on the English version. Latin poetry of the Classical era did not rhyme but the metre was exceedingly strict and some poets, especially Catullus and Horace, experimented with Greek metres which were extremely difficult when transferred to Latin and demanded great technical skill, however simple the final version may appear. It would therefore seem unfair to the memory of these poets not to try to convey something of their technique in a translation. Since rhyme is a traditional method in English poetry of giving a Classical-type pattern and proportion to a work, this has been used where appropriate. In the longer works (especially in Lucretius) emphasis has been put instead on the rolling rhythm and the various figures of speech employed in the original.

B.H.

# Life in Rome

# THE STREETS OF ROME

Here comes the vicious lout,
Sniffing out trouble, drunk,
If he hasn't found someone to knuckle
He's in real agony, sunk
In gloom worse than Achilles mourning his dead
Friend, tossing and turning on his bed -
Otherwise he'd get no sleep at all.
Only one thing makes some men sleep - a brawl.
But even though youth and wine make him run wild,
He'll steer clear of rich folk.
The chap in a scarlet cloak,
With a bodyguard long as your arm,
He'll come to no harm,
Not with his string of torches and his brass lamps.
It's people like me,
Who've only got the moon to see
Me safely home, or short-lived candle light.
(I must be thrifty and watch the wick.)
I'm the one he'll pick.
Hear how the quarrel begins.
Quarrel? It's not a quarrel
When someone else does the beating up
And I just get my shins
Hacked. He stands in your way,
Tells you to stop. You don't dare disobey.
For what can you do
When he's mad and bigger than you?

Then he starts to launch

His attack: 'Where do you come from? That's a fine paunch.

Whose pissy wine and bean-pods are stuffed in there?

What cobbler man's been feeding you

With boiled chap and chopped leek?

What, no answer? Come on, speak,

Beggar man, or I'll kick the life out of you.

Where's your pitch? Some Jewish prayer-shop, I suppose?'

Whether you try to speak or quietly evade his blows,

It's all the same. He'll thrash you in any case.

Then in a rage he says he'll sue.

Yes, if you're poor in Rome you have your due,

Your little freedom: freedom to plead and beg,

When you've been knocked about and punched half dead,

To take back home a few teeth in your head.

JUVENAL, Satire 3, 278 - 301

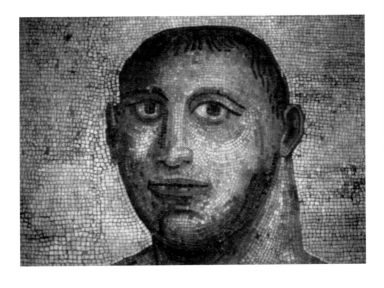

# HIGH RENTS  IN ROME

Down in the Latium villages there are lovely places
(If, of course, you can tear yourself from the races)
That you can buy for what you would have spent
On a black hole in Rome for one year's rent.
Little garden, shallow well - no need to sink
A bucket to give your drooping plants a drink.
Live there and love - your hoe! You'll grow enough at least
To give a horde of vegetarians a feast.
Anywhere, even in the wilds, you'll still prefer
To own one real live worm and be a Grand Seigneur.

JUVENAL, Satire 3, 223 - 231


# MODERN  WOMAN

Abandoning home, husband, sister, ignoring claims
Of country and her children's piteous cries,
She left them to their grief and - here's the surprise -
She left her actor lover and the games.
Though born to ancestral flouncery and lace,
And in downy cradle dreamed her baby dreams,
She mocked the sea, as she mocked the world's esteem.
(With our lounging ladies such scorn is commonplace.)
She faced the Tyrrhenian waves, the Ionian's roar,
Changed one sea for the next and did not quail.
If the cause of danger's chaste - ah! then how frail
The female heart, but once she plays the whore,
Gone the cold fear, the weak, unsteady feet.
Sea travel is cruel if it's a husband's whim -

The bilge makes her sick; the heavens spin and swim.
She'll vomit in his lap and cannot eat.
If a lover invites, it's quite another song:
She's striding the deck and messing with the crew,
Hauling on rough ropes - and laughing too.
It takes adultery to make the stomach strong.

JUVENAL, Satire 6, 85 - 102

## MODERN MARRIAGE

So you've planned a modern marriage: the day is well
And truly fixed; the barber has you groomed;
You've given her a ring, perhaps. - You're doomed.
What snake-haired Fury's hounding you to hell?
Can you endure such slavery? Will you take leave
Of senses, with so much rope around to spare,
High, dizzy windows open to the air,
The Aemilian Bridge on hand to bring reprieve?

JUVENAL, Satire 6, 25 - 32

# AN INVITATION TO DINNER

Fabullus, come round soon to my place to dine
(That is if you don't drop dead).
There'll be a decent spread -
Provided you bring some decent food.
Include a girl (good looker, of course)
And some wine,
And spicy talk for sauce,
And some loud laughs (every possible flavour).
As long as it's a Bring Your Own,
Old charmer, the dinner will be great,
For your friend needs to 'negotiate
A loan.'
      But I'll provide the mood,
Smooth, sophisticated: draughts of love (drunk neat)
For you to savour,
And my special treat,
*Quelque chose*
*De formidable*: a scent
Made by the Love Gods and meant
For my girl. One sniff - so
Marvellous you'll ask the gods to make you grow
All nose.

CATULLUS, 13

# PLEASE FORGET WHAT I SAY

Last night when I'd polished off the third
Bottle, you might have heard
Me invite you to a meal

Today.
Straight away
You thought it was a big deal,
Began jotting
It down, not spotting
I was plain
Sozzled. Never again.
How I detest
A good memory in a fellow guest.

MARTIAL, I. 27

# DON'T DILUTE THE FALERNIAN

Boy, pour me out the dear old stuff,
Strong, dry Falernian, nothing rough,
Just as Postumia's Law decrees.
(She's i/c drinks and boozier than
A boozy grape.) And water, please,
Clear off, go and live with some Puritan.
You only spoil the wine and this
Is undiluted Bacchic bliss.

CATULLUS, 27

15

## DRINK TO THE GIRLS

Let's drink to girls - one good slurp to match
Each letter of their name: for Lyde four,
Justina seven, then five down the hatch
For Lycas; six for Laevia, then three more
For Ida. But as none will come into my bed,
God of Sleep, please come to me instead.

MARTIAL, I. 71

# CURE MY BROKEN HEART

Bacchus, I kneel at your altar with humble prayers.
Grant me a safe journey back to peace.
For Venus has gone mad. Crush her proud airs,
Give healing wine so that love's pains will cease.
For though you marry lovers, yet you can part
Them. Bacchus, wash this weakness from my heart.
If you summon pervading sleep, though temples burn,
I'll cover my hills with vineyards in return.

PROPERTIUS, 3.17, 1 - 6 & 13 - 15

# SOME HOSTS WITH UNPLEASANT HABITS...
# TO A HOST WHO MIXES HIS WINE

Murderer! Does it give you sadistic joy
To poison such a priceless aristocrat
With new wine straight from the vat,
A brew not fit for serving?
What special favours does the rough stuff dispense?
What has the old Falernian done to annoy?
To kill such a body is a criminal offence.
The guests are more deserving:
Kill off a body there and I'll forgive;
But, Tucca, a wine like that deserves to live.

MARTIAL, I. 18

## TO COTTA

You only dine with a man when you've bathed together;
Only the Baths provide you with a guest.
I'm never invited - and so I wonder whether
When I'm naked I don't pass the test.

MARTIAL, I. 23

## TO CAECILIANUS

Only you eat: your guests all watch you feed
As you stuff your guts from mushroom-mountain plate.
What prayer can match such fungus-frenzied greed?
May you eat the sort of mushrooms Claudius ate!

MARTIAL, 1.20

## ......AND A GUEST

Whatever is served, you sweep the table clean -
Sows' teats,
A heathcock just right for two, a roll
Of pork and other dainty meats,
Half a mullet and a pike (whole),
A leg of chicken and a side
Of lamprey, a juicy pigeon in its own sauce -
All these you hide
In your sodden napkin and consign
To your slave to take back home. We others just recline,
Drones in this busy scene.
Have you no remorse?
Put that dinner back. I did not invite
You for a meal *tomorrow* night.

MARTIAL, 2. 37

18

## PRAYER TO AN URN OF WINE

Gracious one, hear me: born in my vintage year
(Manlius was consul) whether you grant us moans
    Or jests, or brawling or wild passion,
        Or easy sleep - by whatever label

Men may address you, guard of choice Massic wine,
Worthy of ritual service on special day,
    Come...urn! Corvinus, seeking smoothness,
        Bids me invite you to join our table.

Thinker he may be, soaked in Socratic talk,
He'll pay you honour, he's not a philistine.
    Wine blends with virtue: there's a rumour
        Even old Cato grew warmer after.

Brains that are dull you put on the sweetest rack,
Press them to wit; you free all the wise man's cares,
    Unlock his hidden, private planning,
        Force him to share it with Bacchus' laughter.

19

You bring back hope to minds that are in distress,
Hearten the poor man, lend him the bull's bold strength;
     After your favours he'll not quake at
        Kings' angry crowns or at armies meeting.

Bacchus and Venus kindly will be your guests,
Joined by the Graces, loath to leave Venus' side;
     Long-burning lamps extend your stay till
        Phoebus' return sets the stars retreating.

HORACE, Odes 3. 21

# PRESENT GIVING

I sent you a little present and though the five day Saturnalia
Has already been and gone,
Yet total failure
To reciprocate -
Not even a minute trinket of tenth-rate
Silver, not even anything handed on,
Like a napkin given to you by a sour-faced
Client, not even a little jar
Of blood-red tuna paste
(I wasn't expecting caviar)
Nor one containing the odd fig
You could hardly call big,
Nor a tiny basket of olives all wizened and rotten,
Just to show that you hadn't forgotten.
All those kind words and smiles: you may get away with it,
But to me you'll always be a blatant hypocrite.

MARTIAL, 4.88

# MORE PRESENT GIVING

The gifts you send to old men and widows are huge.
You'd like me to call you generous, perhaps?
No-one could be a viler, meaner Scrooge.
Only you can call them gifts. They're traps.
So does a treacherous hook tempt fish and so
Are stupid wild beasts deceived by cunning bait.
I'll tell you what 'generous' means, if you don't know:
Give presents to ME - that's how you should donate.

MARTIAL, 4.56

# A WATER SHORTAGE

A vineyard in Ravenna is probably very nice
But I'd rather own a cistern - water's a better price.

MARTIAL, 3. 56

# THE BORE
Linus, you ask what yield my farm returns,
    What revenue.
Linus, the biggest profit that it earns
    Is escaping you.

MARTIAL, 2. 38

## DIRGE ON THE DEATH OF LESBIA'S PET SPARROW

Weep, Venuses and Cupids, weep.
Mourn, every shrine. The bird has gone!
My darling has lost her darling one,
Mourn the sparrow's, the sparrow's sleep.
And men who love loveliness, mourn too.
She loved him more than her own dear eyes.
It was mother-child: he never flew
From her warm breast (that paradise)
But hopped to and fro and chirped his song
To her alone. Now he goes his way
On that dark path (O wicked wrong!)
From which no-one returns, they say.
A curse on you, Death's dark shades, who eat
All lovely things that men enjoy,
You stole that birdie, so honey-sweet.
O dreadful deed! Poor pretty boy!
Yet naughty, too, now you are dead
To make those dear eyes puffy-weepy and red.

CATULLUS, 3

## ISSA THE LAP DOG

Is Issa naughty? An imp, my dear!
Catullus' sparrow's nowhere near.
She's sweeter than the sweetest girl,

22

More precious than an Indian pearl.
(It never stops. It's Issa this
And Issa that.) Issa's kiss
Is chaster and purer than a dove's.
Who is this creature Publius loves?
His darling pretty little peke.
When Issa whines she seems to speak.
Just like us, she's sometimes sad
And sometimes she is oh, so glad.
She sleeps on his neck and curls around
And makes no nasty snoring sound.
So nice is she, at Nature's call
She lets no drop of liquid fall,
Makes no mistakes upon the bed;
With coaxing paw she asks instead
To use her potty. This little maid's
So chaste that she would be afraid
Of Venus: such games are far too rough -
No husband would be good enough.
So that her image will never fade
Publius has had her picture made.
It's more like Issa than she could
Be in actual flesh and blood.
Which one is Issa? - That's the quiz.
This one isn't. Yes it is!
Now both seem painted doggies, now
Each one seems a real bow-wow.

MARTIAL, I. 109

# Love

# HYMN TO VENUS

Venus, mother of Aeneas and Rome, delight
Of gods and men, bounteous, you throng with life
Both vesselled sea and harvest-heavy lands.
Through you each race of creatures is conceived
And springs from darkness to survey the sun.
You come, the winds flee; you come, the clouds retreat.
For you the great sculptor, Earth, raises sweet flowers.
For you the ocean shows only smiling plains
And sky calms her wrath and glows with ungirdled light.
For as soon as the day unveils her face of Spring
And Zephyr's life-fostering breeze, at last unlocked,
Blows free and strong, then first the sky's winged world,
Hearts stirred by your power, announces your approach.
Then herds in lush pastures leap in frenzied joy,
Swim the swift streams, and caught by your charm each one
Follows in eager haste the path you show.
In plundering rivers, seas, on mountain slopes,
In birds' leaf-latticed homes and burgeoning fields,
You strike soft love in every creature's heart
And woo each separate breed to increase its kind.

LUCRETIUS, De Rerum Natura I. 1-20

# LET'S LOVE WHILE WE'RE YOUNG

Love's what life is all about.
Let's love - and treat as trash the store
Of cant when old men moralise.
The sun that sets next day will rise:
One dark unbroken sleep is law
For us, once our brief light goes out.
So kiss in thousands, hundreds, then

26

Hundreds, thousands - and again,
Never counting. Stir them well,
To keep away spite's magic spell,
In case an ill-wisher find the score
And then our kissing game's no more. CATULLUS, 5

## KISSING HUNGER

How many kisses can I take
Before I sicken of such fare?
As many as the countless grains of sand
That lie in that silphium-laden land
From old king Battus' tomb to where
Jove swelters for his oracle's sake.
As many as the still night stars that glow
To spy on men's secret loves below.
Only these, my Lesbia, might appease
My raging hunger, only all these -
Too many for meddlers to count and tell
Or the Evil Tongue to cast its spell. CATULLUS, 7

27

## PROXIMITY

I rank him as a god (or can
Gods reach such heights? - no offence,
    Up there) that man
    Who always has the ritual place,
Hears your soft laughter, gets the close-up view.
    Yet when I do,
I am racked, robbed of sense.
For Lesbia, once I see your face,
    Voice dries - tongue lies
    Numb - fire in limbs
    Sharp, spreading - world swims -
    Ears throb, bells inside -
    Eyes lose sight
        In twice-dyed
           Night.               CATULLUS, 51

## WORDS ON THE WIND

She says she'd choose
To marry me before all others,
    Would refuse
Even Jupiter if he asked.
That's what she says.
    But what a woman says
To a lover who craves
Her embrace should be written on the wind
Or on the coursing waves.

                       CATULLUS, 70

# BATTLE OF HEAD AND HEART

Fool, poor fool, Catullus, still to think
She is yours. Count losses lost. Break clean the link.

Gone are the sunshine days of dazzling light,
Those days when she would choose the path and invite

You to follow. Ah, never again will anyone
Be loved like this. Truly your sun shone.

This was love's laughter time. She made a sport
Of loving, with no lack of willingness to thwart

Your will. Now she says No. So match her pace.
Be firm. No gloom. Be strong. Give up the chase.

Goodbye. Catullus is strong. He will not press,
Will not keep asking when you don't say Yes.

But you'll be sorry later. No-one to adore
You, poor wretch. Unwanted. Think what's in store:
      Who'll come and worship?
      Who'll think you're beautiful?
      Who'll be your next affair?
      Whose name be linked with yours?
      Who'll get your kisses? Whose lips will you tear?
      Who? Who?
      Not you, Catullus, you are strong.
      Not you.

CATULLUS, 8

29

# DON'T RUN AWAY, CHLOE

You're like a little hind
Seeking its anxious mother,
Fleeing from harm,
Paths left behind
In senseless alarm
At even woodland trees.
You would panic at the breeze.

If the faint shiver
Of Spring's arrival
Makes the leaves sway,
Heart and legs quiver.
You'd run away
If the bramble bush part
And a green lizard dart.

I do not pursue
Like a fierce tiger
Or as a lion will.
I hunt to woo,
Not crush and kill.
Time to seek your safe place
In a lover's embrace.

HORACE, Odes I. 23

# GOODBYE TO PYRRHA

Who is it now, Pyrrha?
    What slim-hipped boy
        In some enchanted cave
           On layers of roses
      Breathes his wave
        Of sensuous scents
           To urge you to joy?

Whose treat to watch you tie
        That yellow hair
                With simple art?
                        What tears he'll shed
        For Faith's changed heart
                And fickle gods,
                        Still unaware

Of treacherous winds!  How he will gape
        At storm-black seas!
                Now he basks in rays
                        Of gold, foresees a length
        Of cosy, squall-free days.
                What trust, what innocence!
                        Unhappy these

Who idly think your sun will always shine.
        I've furled my sails,
                Retired, and made my vow
                        To Neptune: his temple wall
        Shows I have offered now
                My shipwrecked clothes and said
                        Farewell to gales.

HORACE, Odes I. 5

# WHY SO SILENT, FLAVIUS?

Flavius, your latest amour
Must be a pretty poor
Specimen of charm and wit,
An ordinary little bit,
Otherwise you would tell
Catullus all about her. (Like hell
You would.) But you've fallen for a tart. Yes,
A temperature-raising tart - and are ashamed to confess.
But though you'd like to keep it mum,
Like to lay claim
To celibate nights,
Your bed isn't dumb
And will squeak
On you. The garlands, the reek
Of Syrian unguent and here and there
The signs of wear
Are proof enough. Your bed cites,
Will make a witty speech that's incriminatory,
A shaky frame,
But the style rhythmic and ejaculatory.
So why this silence? Why disguise
Debauchery? Your thinning thighs
Show you've been up to silly tricks. No more bluff.
With tit-bits of what was nice and what wasn't you could stuff -
A poem of mine. I'll
Elevate
You and your beloved to the divine state.
At least my verse has style.

CATULLUS, 6

# DIDO ACCUSES AENEAS OF DESERTING HER

Traitor ! So concealment was your plan, to hide
So great a wrong and in stealth and silence leave our land.
Did not our love, did not the hand you gave in pledge,
Did not the thought that cruel death would be your Dido's fate
Detain you? Can you be toiling at the fleet
When winter's stars still shine? Is your cruel heart
So eager to cross the deep amid the northern gales?
You sail in search of foreign lands and unfamiliar homes.
But even if ancient Troy still stood, would you still sail
To Troy over such a raging sea? You seek escape.
From me? I beg you by these tears and by that promise
You gave me - for my own folly has left me no other plea,
Left only misery - by our union, by those solemn vows
We both had undertaken, if you remember any kindnesses,
If ever you have a happy thought of me, I beg again
Show pity for the downfall of my home and if there is still room
For pleas, shed your unworthy plan. Because of you
The tribes of Africa and the Nomad rulers hate me
And even my Tyrians are now my foes. Because of you
My honour has been killed and that fair name of old,
My only path to everlasting glory. Can you so leave me,
With only Death to care for me, my - guest? No other name
Is left to me, though husband was ever on my lips.
Why should I linger in this life and wait for my brother
Pygmalion to destroy my walls, or Gaetulian Iarbas
To drag me off to marriage? At least if I had conceived your child
Before your flight, a little Aeneas playing in my  hall,
Who by his looks would bring you back to me, I should not feel
I had been so betrayed, so utterly forsaken.

VIRGIL, Aeneid 4, 305 - 330

# NEOBULE'S LAMENT

Pity the lovesick girl!  Forbidden to give free play
To love, forbidden to let wine's sweetness wash away
    Its pangs, her fate to swoon in fright
    At whiplash tongue of guardian male,

Her lot the loom. But oh, Neobule, the winged boy with his dart
Steals your wool-basket, steals concentration on Minerva's toilsome art,
    If he once give brief sight
    Of Hebrus' beauty, born in Greek-tale

Isle.  To bathe in rippling Tiber watch him strip!
Watch him surpass Bellerophon in horsemanship!
    (Those varnished shoulders gleaming bright)
    His fist and swift foot can never fail.

Skilled too in the hunt, to shoot the herd of startled deer
Over the open plain; and facing his quick spear
    As it lurks in crackling thicket site,
    Even the wild boar will quail.

HORACE, Odes 3. 12

# LOVE'S  MEDALS

Messalla, you are suited to campaigns,
You wage heroic wars on land and sea
So that your house may boast your battle gains.
A lover's medals are the ones for me.
If I am taken prisoner, let the chains
In beauty's ambush trap me willingly.

If I stand guard, I'll watch hard-hearted doors -
Glory and accolades are not my aim.
Delia, if I can share my life with yours,
The slur of sloth and ease will be no shame,
And in my last hour, when life's sweet strength withdraws,
Your smile, your touch are solaces I'll claim.
Meanwhile let's yoke our love while fate allows;
Soon will come dark-cowled Death with noiseless tread;
Now is the time for lovers' games and vows,
Now let the pleas and wooing words be said.
Love's quarrels will not suit our greying brows,
She shrinks to break down doors when youth is fled.
Here will I fight and play the general's part,
In love will I act the soldier and be brave.
Trumpets, begone and battle flags, depart:
Bring wounds and wealth to valiant men who crave
You. Safe with the riches stored within my heart,
To money or hunger I'll not be a slave.

TIBULLUS, 1.1, 52-59, 68-78

## TO DELIA

My tone was harsh: parting was something, I said, that I could bear.
    Now my brave boasting is far behind me.
Imagine a top kept spinning on flat ground, by a boy lent speed
    By his long-practised art. So am I whipped along.
Torture this creature here with fire and screw, so that grand talk
    May never please again. Tame the beast's bristling words.
Yet spare him, too, I beg, by the bonds of that secret bed,
    By the joys of love and our two heads lying close.
Think when you once lay sick, exhausted by that terrible disease:

35

They say it was I who saved you by my prayers,
  Letting the crone first chant her magic spell, then with my own hands
    Offering gifts of cleansing sulphur round your bed.
Who paid due homage to your cruel dreams, to purge their power to harm
    Appeasing them three times with sacred meal?
Who wore the woollen fillet on his brow and in loose robes
    Made the nine vows to Trivia at dead of night?
All these rites I performed: but now another enjoys my love,
    His luck to reap the blessings of my prayers.


I pictured a life of happiness, if only you were spared.
    Fool. A god said No. I'll till my land.
Delia will help (I thought) and guard the grain while the threshing-floor
    Treads out the harvest in the blazing sun.
Or she will keep safe my grapes in their brimming troughs
    As the gleaming must is crushed by flying feet.
She'll soon grow used to counting the flock, will train the prattling
    Slave-child to play on its loving mistress' lap.
She'll learn what gifts are due to the god of farms; in return for vines
    Some grapes, for corn some ears, for the flock a solemn feast.
Let her be queen of the farm, of work and workers all,
    My joy to be a cipher in the house.
My dear Messalla shall visit and Delia shall offer him
    Sweet fruits, pulling them down from chosen trees.
She shall respect such glory, busily tend his needs,
    Prepare a feast and wait on him herself.


These were my dreams and prayers but the East Wind and the South
    Toss them across Armenia's scented land.
Often I tried to drive away my cares with drink
    But grief kept turning all the wine to tears.
Often I embraced a different girl, but on the brink of bliss
    Venus said, 'Remember the other one,' and left.
The girl would go, shamefaced, would say I was bewitched

And spread the tale my Delia knew occult arts.
But Delia does not cast her spell by words: her face, her soft arms
      Are her magic, and her golden hair -
Like Thetis, the sea-nymph, who in days of old bridled a fish
      And rode all gleaming blue to Peleus.
Yet her charms have served me ill. A rich lover is now in train.
      The cunning bawd has schemed my tragic end.
May the meal she eats be blood and with gore-stained lips
      May she drink from cups made bitter with draughts of gall.
May ghosts flit around her, continually bemoaning their fate,
      And the vampire bird screech frantically from her roof.
Let her feel hunger's goad, go mad in search for weeds on graves
      And bones which savage wolves have left behind.
Let her run bare-bellied and shrieking through the towns and
                      then be chased
      From crossroads by a furious pack of dogs.
It will happen. A god predicts it. A lover has his special deities.
      Venus is angry if scorned and her laws misused.


So quick, make haste, forget the teachings of the grasping witch.
      Gifts don't bring victory in the battle for love.
A poor man is ever hovering to serve, a poor man will be the first
      To pay you court and stay at your defenceless side.
A poor man will be a trusty friend in a jostling crowd,
      Will use his hands profitably to find a way.
A poor man will take you unobserved to secret friends
      And himself pull the sandals from your snow-white feet.
Alas! my verse is in vain. Her door is shut and will not yield to words.
      The hand that knocks on it must not be empty.
But you who are now her favourite, beware the fate that was mine;
      Fortune is fickle. Her wheel spins swiftly round.
Not without reason does the man now standing patiently at her door
      Survey the ground ahead and then retreat;
Pretend to pass her house, then quickly run back all alone

And just as he enters, interminably clear his throat.
Love likes stealth. She has some scheme afoot, enjoy it, please,
While you can. Your boat still sails calm seas.

TIBULLUS, 1. 5

# TO CYNTHIA

## ENCHANTMENT

Beloved, a lucky omen marked your birth:
The Love God in all his glory sneezed aloud.
Such gifts are not from a mother of this earth
But from the gods; your splendour is heaven-endowed.
That spell within the womb's too short for gracing
One with a city's homage as her due,
First of Rome's daughters to know Jove's embracing,
(We'll reach Olympian heights together too).
The beauty that Helen wore is come again:
What cause for wonder if my youthful fire
Burns strong? Much nobler had Troy fallen then,
For Cynthia's sake. 'How could a girl inspire
The clash of continents beneath Troy's citadel?' -
I used to say of Menelaus' hate
For Paris. But now I understand too well
The one's insistence, the other's fight for mate.

## DISENCHANTMENT

Woman, that faith in your beauty is unfounded,
Your pride fed fat on the fondness of my eyes;
With Love's blind tributes my verses were compounded.

Now I feel shame I could so idealise.
I often praised your beauty's contrasting fashion,
Compared your complexion with the dawn's clear light,
Viewed you from the dreamland of my passion.
Reality shows chalk counterfeit of white.
Old friends could not steer me from my madman's track,
No magic-woman cleanse me in Ocean's flow;
I confessed my folly (no need for rod or rack)
Wrecked in a wide Aegean sea of woe.
My hands were manacled and I was caught
In Love's cruel melting-pot. But see: at last
My flower-decked prow proclaims me safe in port,
The quicksands crossed, the anchor firmly cast.
Now health and sanity once more are mine,
My wearying fever passed, my flesh close healed.
Accept, Good Sense, my service at your shrine.
To all my prayers Jove's ears were always sealed.

PROPERTIUS, 2.3. 23-38 & 3. 24

# GIRLS:  A CONFESSION

Hear my confession: mine not the saintly role.
    I would not dare to use
An armoury of lies. My sins are large;
    I have no just excuse.
And having confessed (confession soothes the soul)
    I'm suddenly ablaze
To enter battle and to lead the charge
    Against my wicked ways.
I hate what I am but cannot not be so.

I'm longing to discard
My vices, but my will won't operate.
　　Ah me! The burden's hard.
I'm like a little skiff tossed to and fro.
　　Alas, I don't require
A special type of looks to titillate -
　　All girls arouse desire.
This one is modest, glances demurely down:
　　Her innocence ensnares
And I'm on fire. That one knows the ropes,
　　Displays her many wares.
I love a girl who likes the streets of town
　　And isn't country-bred;
Sophisticated manners offer hopes
　　Of pliancy in bed.
Another seems strict and puts on old-fashioned looks:
　　I know it's all an act;
There'll be no resistance when my amorous schemes
　　Are deftly turned to fact.
You may be blessed with brains and steeped in books -
　　You're still the girl for me.
Darling, you're dumb - I love you for what seems
　　Charming simplicity.
Another likes my poems, thinks they're urbane
　　And far outshine the Greeks'.
I love her. Why? Because she loved me first.
　　There's yet another who speaks
Of both my work and talent with disdain,
　　Says I'm no laureate.
I love her, though the position's now reversed
　　And long to bear the weight
Of - just her guilt, of course. Another will show
　　Softly swinging hips.
I'm hooked; but if she's stiff I'm still on fire.

A man can give her some tips.
This one sings sweetly: as she trills her lah-te-doh
    I'll kiss each note. How I'm thrilled
At seeing nimble fingers pluck the lyre.
    I love it when hands are skilled.
If you're too tall, no matter, I equate
    You with Amazons in strength
And heroines of old; what's more your size
    Will match the bed in length.
If you're too small, you'll still accommodate.
    Both long and short will wreck
My virtuous vows and soon demoralise.
    Black locks on snowy neck
Entice me: Leda was dark and made her catch
    (They say it was a swan).
The one with golden tresses I shall claim
    Is goddess of Dawn.
Give me the girl, I'll find a myth to match.
    Is she young and pure?
Then she'll disturb. She'll do so just the same
    If she is more mature.
The filly's fine flesh, the mare's a better ride
    And also quicker home.
And when a Minister of Love's required
    To rule those girls in Rome
Judged to be generally on the pretty side,
    How could I not win?
I'll canvass for their favours, still untired,
    And know they'll vote me in.

OVID, Amores 2. 4

1-28, 33-36, 41-48

## APOLLO FALLS IN LOVE WITH DAPHNE

Daphne was first to touch Apollo's heart,
Given not by Chance, but Cupid's angry dart.
The God of Delos, filled with a victor's pride
At crushing Delphi's python, had espied
The little Love God stretching his bowstring tight
And said, 'You are just a child at play. What right
Have you to wield a warrior's arms? They match
Our shoulders better. Our valour can despatch
With unerring wounds wild beast and human foe;
Our shower of arrows recently laid low
The bloated python till it sank the rage

Of its poisonous belly over vast acreage.
Your weapon is the torch: enough if its flame
Kindles some little loves. Do not lay claim
To honours fit for me.' Cupid's words were few:
'Your shaft may pierce the whole world. Mine will pierce you.
Just as a god excels all living things,
Our fame surpasses yours.' He shook his wings
And darted nimbly through the air to seek
A vantage point on Parnassus' shady peak.
There he drew from his quiver's teeming load
Two arrows with different roles - the one to goad
The other to rout love; the one was shining gold
With sharpened point, the other of blunter mould,
Its shaft lead-tipped. With this the god took aim
At Daphne; the other pierced Apollo's frame
Until it travelled through to his very core.
At once he loved; her shaft made her abhor
The very name of love. The forest lairs
Of beasts were now her chief delight, and snares
And hunting spoils. Her virgin ardour vied
With the goddess Diana's, her lawless hair was tied
By a single ribbon.
              Many sought her hand.
She roamed the trackless woods, shunning the band
Of suitors, impatient of man's desires, and free,
Not caring what Hymen and wedded love might be.
Her father chided: 'A son-in-law is my due.'
Then, pressing her: 'You owe me grandsons too.'
She hated the marriage torch as something base
And modest blushes stained her lovely face.
Encircling his neck with coaxing arms, she cried:
'Dearest father, let me not be denied
The joys of everlasting maiden bliss.
Diana's father once allowed her this.'

Her father succumbed. But Daphne, your beauty's power
Forbade the fulfilment of your wish. Your dower
Of loveliness ill-suited such a plea.
Apollo saw, loved, and wooed her instantly.
His prophetic gifts deceived his hopeful heart.
As in a harvested field a blaze will start
Amid the light stubble; or as a hedge will burn
From a fire which some traveller's unconcern
Has kindled too close, or left at break of day
To smoulder unnoticed while he goes his way,
So was the god on fire: his whole heart blazed.
He fed his barren love with hope; he gazed
At her hair now tumbling loose upon her neck,
Imagined her beauty if she were to deck
Those tresses. He saw her star-bright eyes, he saw
Her lovely lips, and seeing, begged for more.
Fingers, hands, arms, the naked curve
Of shoulders thrill him; the hidden parts all serve
To make him think them lovelier.
                              She sped away
Fast as the fleeting breeze and did not stay
To hear the Sun God's words: 'Nymph, do not flee.
Do not flee, I pray, it is no enemy
That chases you. So does the lamb take fright
At wolf, the deer at lion; in trembling flight
The dove flees the eagle. For me it is love which fires
The chase. Alas, do not fall and let the briars
Scar those blameless limbs. Let me not cause pain.
The region where you run is rough: restrain
Your flight and slacken your pace. I too will ease
Pursuit. But ask whose heart it is you please.
I am no mountain shepherd of the wild,
Guarding the flocks and herds. Impetuous child,
You do not know your lover, so you flee.
Delphi, Claros, Tenedos bow to me,

Patara's realms too. From Jupiter my descent.
I gave to man's songs the lyre accompaniment.
My arrow flies straight (but another's, straighter than mine,
Wounded a heart unaware of Love's design).
Through me past, present, future are revealed.
Through my discoveries sickness is healed.
The world calls me Saviour. Herbs are in my control.
Alas, that none of these can render whole
My love-sick heart, that none of all my skills
Can cure their master, though they cure others' ills.'

He would have continued with his résumé
Of talents but she pursued her frightened way
And left both god and unsaid words behind.
Still she looked beautiful: the wind outlined
Her figure and as she ran into the breeze
Its gentle impulse fluted her draperies
And wafted her hair. No more was the god content
To waste his youthful passion on blandishment.
Love forced his pace: as when a Gallic hound
Sights a hare upon the open ground.
The one seeks safety in speed, the other his catch.
Hound seems to have his quarry,  hopes to attach,
With thrusting muzzle grazing her footprints; hare
Streaks from his snapping jaws, and unaware
If she is caught or not, strives to evade
The encroaching fangs. Just so run god and maid.

But now the god ran faster, gave her no rest,
Helped by love's wings; his menacing ardour pressed
Hard on her fleeing heels. Her strength was spent
And pale from the fright of her predicament,
As she felt his breath upon her tumbling hair,
She saw her father's stream and gasping a prayer,
Collapsed. 'Father, bring help and if in your waves

There dwells some river deity that saves,
Change and destroy this form with which I pleased
Too well.' Scarce had she finished - a numbness seized
Her limbs, around her breast a delicate layer
Of bark evolved, her arms reached for the air
And soared into branches, hair became leaves, each foot
That lately strove for speed, took clinging root.
Yet even now, though human head had gone,
From the tree-top image her loveliness still shone.
Still the god loved her and touching the stem, could tell
Her heart still fluttered under its new-formed shell.
He locked arms round branches as if they were flesh, and sank
Kisses upon the wood: the wood still shrank.
At last, 'Ah, since you cannot be my bride,
At least as a tree you will be mine,' he cried.
'My hair, my lyre, my quiver shall from this day
Always possess you - as a wreath of bay.
Victorious Roman generals you shall attend,
When Capitol sees the long train ascend
And hears glad voices raise the Triumph song.
There, at Augustus' portals, trusty and strong,
You will guard the civic oak that stands between,
And just as my locks are unshorn and evergreen,
So shall your leafy glory never fade.'

The Healing God had finished: the laurel swayed,
Waving her new-made branches' ornament
And nodding her tree-top head as if in consent.

OVID, Metamorphoses I. 452 - 567

46

# MARRIED LOVE

## CEPHALUS AND PROCRIS
(Cephalus relates the story)

What pleasure to recall wedlock's first stage, that happy span,
    The marriage norm,
When man finds his bliss in wife and wife her bliss in man;
    When to perform
Each for each those acts of loving care was joy for us two;
    When no other name
Could lure - not even should Venus ask or Jupiter woo.
    An equal flame
Burned in both hearts. As soon as the morning sun struck his first blow,
    Shooting his rays
On hill-tops, waking the grain of youth, then I would go
    My forest ways
To hunt. I took no horses, no knotted nets, no escort band
    Of beaters, no scent
Of sniffing hounds. My javelin was my defence. When my right hand
    Was more than content

With slaughter of the wild, seeking cool shade, in my flushed state
    I wooed the breeze,
That gentle breeze which came from the chill vales. There I would wait
    To find that ease
After toil which only she could give. 'Breeze,' I would cry,
    (Now I recall
My words) 'Come, soothe me, come to my welcoming arms to pacify
    (For you can) this all-
Consuming heat.' I might perhaps have added, such is Fate's mesh,
    Another few
Endearments: 'You are my greatest joy' or 'You refresh
    And comfort, you
Make me love the woods and lonely places. My lips ever long
    (I may have said)
To catch your breath.' Someone heard and caught the words' wrong
    Strand, misled
By their double meaning; thought the name which I so often used,
    That name of 'Breeze',
Belonged to a nymph, believed I loved a nymph and straightway accused.
    My infamies,
All false, the informer whispered in Procris' ear in eagerness.
    Love believes anything.
Swooning from sudden grief (they say) Procris fell spiritless.
    Recovering
At last, she proclaimed her misery, proclaimed her fate unkind,
    Lamented my
Bad faith, fearing a name which had body only in her mind,
    Demented by
The groundless charge, grieving as if her rival had existence.
    Yet some relief
She gave her misery by doubts, and hopes, and by resistance
    To belief
In tell-tale words, rejecting her husband's sins, refusing to indict
    Unless  her eyes

Had seen them. As soon as the next day's dawn had driven back night,
    I arise
And leave for the woods. Triumphant from the hunt, I call 'Come near,
    Breeze, and calm
My weariness.' And even as I spoke I seemed to hear
    A vague alarm,
A kind of groan. Still I continued, 'Come, loveliest of all.'
    As my words ceased,
Again that slight rustling caused by a leaf's faint fall.
    Thinking a beast
Was lurking there, I suddenly hurled my fast-flying
    Javelin. No!
No beast - but Procris, clutching her breast's deep wound and crying
    Her heart's woe.
When once I recognised the voice of my faithful wife,
    Wildly I sped
In frenzied haste towards that voice, to find her life
    Half fled,
Her clothes spattered and stained with blood. Her own sweet gift,
    (Sad irony)
The javelin she gave me, she was drawing from her wound. I lift
    That form, to me
Dearer than my own, in gentle arms. I tore
    Her robe, and
Bound her cruel wound to staunch the blood, and implore
    Her not to brand
Me by her death, not to desert me. She now lacked
    All strength, but said
These few words, forcing her dying lips: 'By that pact
    Of our marriage bed,
By all the gods of heaven and of my home, I plead and pray,
    By all that I
Offered you in kindness, by the love that still stays strong today,
    When I now die,

Do not let that Breeze share the marriage that is ours.'
　　　Then at last
I realised and explained. But what use now to explain? Her powers
　　　Were ebbing fast
Along with her blood. As long as she had strength to fix her eyes
　　　On anything,
She fixed them on me. My lips are there to carry, as it dies,
　　　Her suffering
Spirit. Her last look was happier. She seemed content. Weeping,
　　　This history
Cephalus told to all. We answered with our tears, keeping
　　　Him company.

OVID, Metamorphoses 7, 797 - 863

## TO HIS WIFE

Dear wife, let us keep through life our love's strong thread,
And may no day arrive to change our hearts' ways;
Preserve the names of earliest marriage bed,
Mirrored as youthful lovers all our days.
Though I may span more time than Homer's sage
And your years exceed the ancient Sibyl's goal,
May we never know the habit of old age.
Better to count Time's favours than its toll.

AUSONIUS

Oxford Book of Latin Verse 328

50

# The Countryside

# CHOOSING A COW

A cow will show her mettle by her mould:
Best is thick neck and ugly head, and lank
From her chin, to skim her legs, a lapping fold
Of skin should hang; then look for sweep of flank
That has no limit set. Let all be vast scale,
Feet too. Choose shaggy ears and inward hook
Of horn. A cow is to my taste with pale
Markings, who will throw the yoke, will look
More like a bull; will all her length walk tall
And brush her footprints with her tail's low fall.

VIRGIL, Georgics 3. 50-59

# A COUNTRY FESTIVAL TO THE GOD FAUNUS

Faunus, who give chase when the wood-nymph runs,
Walk soft through my fields and sunny lands,
Leave my young sheep, my foster sons,
　　　Blessed by your hands.

Your old altar will smoke with its fragrant debt
Of incense, a tender kid be killed,
Love's comrade, the wine-bowl, will brim and let
　　　Your due be spilled.

The year now is full: your feast day will see
The meadows filled with dallying flocks,
The village share its festivity
　　　With leisured ox;

See lambs without fear as the wolf roams round,
The wood in your honour its leaves deploy,
The ditch-digger dance on his foe, the ground,
　　　With pounding joy.

HORACE,  Odes 3. 18

# FIGHTING FOR A MATE

The bulls spy her grazing deep in Sila's wood,
The lovely heifer. At once they engage with thrust
And wound and answering thrust and wound; black blood
Floods their bodies and all the clashing lust
Is forced into the bellowing rivalry

Of horns. The woods and high heaven return the roar.
No sharing now of meadows' tenancy,
But loser is exiled to a foreign shore,
Lowing his shame at wounded flesh and pride,
At love renounced and vengeance languishing,
His wistful eyes on pasturage denied
As he leaves the land where all his sires were king.
So now his only care to train for deeds
Of strength, through the long night his bed austere
On rocks. In practice frays his diet of reeds,
Sword-edged, and prickly leaves helps him to steer
His fury into his horns. Soon he has gored
The tree-trunks, lunged at the winds. Now see him throw
Up sand in prelude, then, vigour and power restored,
Bearing the colours, charge his unwary foe.

VIRGIL, Georgics 3. 219 - 236

# A SPRING IN THE COUNTRYSIDE

    Bandusian Spring,
Tomorrow we honour your crystal stream
    And sparkling grace.
    Sweet wine, a flower offering
And feast-day homage from the frisking herd
    Our tribute in due place.


    The gentle swelling
On the young kid's brow, the early horns,
    Are nature's prophecy,
    Fighting-for-mate foretelling.

Your cool stream's crimson stain will prove
    His unfinished destiny.

    Your healing power
Stays ever sure, untouched by
    The Dog-Day burning
    Of Sirius' cruel hour.
You refresh the ox, exhausted by the plough,
    And cattle returning.

    You too will share
The fame of other springs, when I have praised
    Your oak tree's shade,
    Your grottoed mouth, from where
Your lavish flow leaps eloquently forth
    In chattering cascade.

HORACE, Odes 3. 13

55

# BEES

They live their lives by their distinctive code,
Sharing their sons and honouring their nation state,
Building their cities as one common abode.
They have fixed household gods to venerate,
And they alone. They harvest summer's yields,
Remembering winter, obeying their mighty laws,
Toiling by treaty. Some forage in the fields
And hoard for the general good their hard-won stores;
Others, within the fences of their homes,
Stack up narcissus tears and tree-trunk's ooze
To lay the first foundations of their combs,
And hang in the hive their special resinous glues.
Some train the young, new promise of the race,
Some store the liquid nectar and inflate
The cells and pack pure honey into place.
For other bees their lot to guard the gate,
Spy out the rains in turn if skies are dull,
Lift homecomers' loads and now, in soldier mime,
Keep out the lazy drones. The air is full
Of buzz and bustle and the scent of thyme.
Just as the Cyclops (if one can compare
The epic with the small) in confederate craft
With bull's-hide bellows take and return the air
And speed the slow metal for Jove's thunder-shaft,
Dip hissing sheets of bronze in Etna's lakes,
Lift up their arms as one in rhythmic might,
Hammer the anvil till the mountain quakes,
Manage the metal, gripped in the forceps' bite;
So do the bees, impelled by nature's spur,
Her drive to do, fulfil their destined role;
In rest and labour young and old concur
In nature's plan for one harmonious whole.
Ordering the cities is the old bees' care:
They fortress the combs and mould the fretted wall.
The young throughout the meadows play their share

56

Among the silvery willow pastures. All
Rush from the gates at daybreak, pollen bent,
Seeking wild strawberries and the fragrant bark,
Rich lime flowers and the rust-red corn-flag's scent,
Bright crocus blooms. When evening sets its mark
On feasting and reminds them it is late,
They head for home to restore their flagging limbs,
Wearied from working and their thymy freight.
They seek the hive's chinks and hum around the rims.
The low-toned murmurs ever louder grow.
Soon in their chambers they settle in their beds,
Limbs numbed in sleep that only they can know.
Far into night a stately silence spreads.

VIRGIL, Georgics 4 153 - 190

## THE EAGLE

Gold against the crimson sky flew Jupiter's great-winged bird,
Chasing the whirring line of sea-shore birds and all its squawking
                                                            troop,
When suddenly he swooped towards the waves, a monstrous
                                                            shadow,
And in his talons' clutch he seized a prize swan. The Italians stared
In wonder at the marvellous sight: for all the retreating band
With shrieking war-cry wheeled their flight and darkening the sky
                                                            with wings,
Formed up and sent their battle cloud charging against the foe
Until, forced by their onslaught and his burden's weight, he
                                                            weakened.
Then in mid-air he dropped his prey out of his talons' grasp
Into the current and fled into the hinterland of cloud.

VIRGIL, Aeneid 12, 247-256

57

## THE WOLF

He slinks from the kill, this time a shepherd or a giant steer,
Away before attacking weapons can pursue, and strikes
A lonely path up to the tallest hills, there to hide.
And sensing his guilt, his too bold deed, he thrusts his throbbing tail
Between his legs to stroke and soothe his belly, and heads for the woods.

VIRGIL, Aeneid 11, 809 - 813

## THE SNAKE

From the base of the shrine came a snake,
slippery, huge,
Trailing seven loops and seven twisting coils;
It quietly embraced the tomb then glided between the altars.
His blue-branded back shone bright and spangled splendour
Burnished his scales with gold, like a rainbow that fronts the sun
And flings on the clouds a thousand different colours.

VIRGIL, Aeneid 5, 84 - 89

58

# PLAGUE KILLS AN OX

Suddenly he falls, in his cruel share's own groove,
Still steaming, coughs blood and foam from his stricken breast
Nor waits for the grieving ploughman to remove
The heavy yoke, but groans to his final rest.
The plough lies lonely where in mid-task it stayed.
Loud is the mourning of his brother ox.
No longer will he know the tall woods' shade,
Soft meadows, and the stream which leaps the rocks,
Speeding clear as amber to the plain.
Such joys with one long last flank-shuddering breath
Are gone; his eyes grow dull, he looks in vain,
Lays down his neck and droops his weight to death.
And now what help the ploughing and the toil?
What help those many kindly acts of grace?
What help to have upturned the heavy soil?
Yet nothing in his simple life was base.
Luxury does not corrupt the beasts
With loaded tables, gifts of Bacchic wealth;
Their wine clear springs, swift streams, and grass their feasts.
No worries break the unclouded sleep of health.

VIRGIL, Georgics 3, 515 - 530

# THE LANGUAGE OF ANIMALS

Why should we wonder if the human race,
Owners of expressive voice and tongue,
Used varying tones to fit its varying moods,
When even dumb cattle and the wild beast brood

All summon forth distinct and different sounds
For fear, and grief, and swelling surge of joy?
See, the facts tell us clearly this is so.
When Molossian hounds are baring cruel teeth,
With great soft gaping jowls grinning with rage
And snarling angry threats, how different the tone
From natural bark which fills the whole air with sound.
Again, when they lick their pups with loving tongue,
Toss them with their paws, then reach to bite,
Staging a gentle game of gobbling up
And checking their clenching teeth, then how remote
Are those fond whimpers of delight from that
Loud howling when left lonely in the house
Or whining for mercy as they cringe and crouch
To avoid a master's blows.
                     With horses too
Listen when the stallion in his prime
Runs raging among the mares, pricked by winged love's
Sharp spurs; listen when with nostrils wide
He snorts out his eager frenzy for the fight.
Do you not hear a very different sound
From when a normal neighing shakes his frame?
The family of winged and flying things,
Hawks, and ospreys, and gulls that forage for food
And life amid the salt sea-waves, all change
Their cries. Not always do you hear the shrieks
That signal they are squabbling over food
And thwarting plunder. Some match their harsh-toned songs
To moods of weather: in bird lore flocks of rooks
And long-lived ravens often call the rain
And sometimes cry for winds and breezes too.
Therefore if different feelings drive the beasts,
Dumb though they are, to utter different cries,

How much more reasonable that early man
Could label different things by different sounds.

LUCRETIUS, De Rerum Natura 5, 1056 - 1090

# THE SHEPHERD DISPOSSESSED BY CIVIL WAR

Melibous:

Lucky old man!
There among familiar streams and nymph-hallowed springs
You'll chase the cool shade. Here the hedge
Down by your neighbour's fields will yet another year
Feed your noble bees with its willow blooms, their gentle
Hum coaxing you to enter the land of sleep; and there
Under that tall rock the vine dresser as he prunes
Will sing to the sky. And all the while your throaty pigeons
Will bring you your special joy, and still the turtle dove
Will send her soft cooing from the high-branching elm.
But some of us must go, off to the thirsty Africans
Or else to Scythia, others until we reach
The Cretan river's swift, chalk-rolling stream,
And some to the distant Britons, divorced by the whole world's
breadth.
Shall I in days to come ever know again
The fields where I was born, my humble cottage roof,
Stacked high with turf, and thrill to see the ears of corn,
That kingdom of my own? This land I ploughed and husbanded
So carefully, shall an uncaring soldier have?
A foreigner own these crops? Ah, to what misery

61

Discord has brought us Romans! Is it for men like these
We sowed our fields? Now graft your pears, Melibous,
Now plant your vines in rows. Go, my goats, go.
Once you were a happy herd. Nevermore
Shall I lie stretched in a green hollow and see you
Far off, hanging from the bramble-matted crags.
No more songs shall I sing, never drive you, goats,
To crop the flowering clover and the savoury willow shoots.

Tityrus:

But still, you could stay here this one night with me, and sleep
On green leaves. I have some apples newly ripe,
Some tender chestnuts and a store of creamy cheese.
Already the roof-tops of the distant farm are trailing
Smoke, and shadows fall longer from the tallest hills.

VIRGIL, Eclogue I, 51-58 & 64-83

# THE FARMER'S LIFE IS BEST

The man who in lust for power has stained his hand
With brothers' blood must seek a foreign sun,
Change his dear homestead for a different land
And lonely exile. The farmer's work is done
With curving ploughshare, cutting his native soil.
This is his life, this gives the year's reward,
Not looted palaces and cities' spoil.
From here his sons and grandsons have their board,
His herds of oxen and his faithful steer.

Nature can never rest: the sheaves of wheat,
The fruits, the flock's bounty all enrich the year;
Lush produce fills the plough's wake and heaps defeat
On barns. Then winter comes: the olive mill
Keeps grinding and prize acorns fall for swine
To take glad bellies home; wild berries spill.
Autumn teems in her turn: the fresh-stripped vine
Ripens its clusters high on a sunny rock.

His home is chaste and follows virtue's ways.
On his return his precious children flock
To hang on his kisses. His cattle graze
With bursting udders. His fields are rich and green
And fatten his young goats to proud display
Of sparring horns in lusty battle scene.
Lord of all this, he keeps his holiday.
His friends wreathe Bacchus' bowl around the flames;
He pours the wine, invites his rustic realm
To try its archer's skill in shepherd games
And hangs a target from his favourite elm.
Then, stripping work-hardened muscles, they contest
In wrestling bouts.                    This life our forbears led,
This life to the early Sabine folk seemed best.
To such a life our founder twins were bred.
In this Etruria's power had its birth.
Here were our seeds of greatness: Rome grew tall
And came to be the fairest thing on earth,
Uniting her seven hills within a wall.

                              VIRGIL,  Georgics 2, 510-535

# Travel
# and Places

## SPRING WANDERLUST

The soft airs of returning Spring
    And Winter thawed
Quicken the soul's sharp hungering
    To range abroad.
Now Zephyr's sensuous winds dispel
    The wild March sky;
Asia's bright cities cast their spell,
    There let us fly.
Forsake Nicaea's sultry heat,
    The plains of Troy,
An eager throbbing stirs the feet
    With promised joy.
Yet what of sweet friendship now survives?
    Together from Rome,
Now different paths of changing lives
    Take us back home.

CATULLUS, 46

## RETURNING HOME TO SIRMIO

Of headlands and islands all that ride
Whether on Neptune's oceantide
Or on his still lakes, the loveliest I know,
Is you, my little Sirmio.
Oh, 'Good to see you!' and 'Glad to be here!'
And 'Can it be true?' Am I really clear
Of Thynia and the Bithynian plain?
Are we both safe and meet again?
Care banished is a blessed state:

The burdened mind can shed the weight
Of wandering and pay the rites
To god of home and restful nights
In long-missed bed. Just this one thing
Repays for all past suffering.
Welcome me, Sirmio, with chattering slaves,
With laughter that ripples from Garda's waves,
Laughter that bursts behind your doors:
Your master's here and he is yours.                    CATULLUS, 31

## CATULLUS' YACHT

That yacht you see there, friends, will speak
And state her case:
'I was the swiftest vessel on the seas -
No sprint by any timber-strake afloat
But I could outpace,
Whether I worked the breeze
With oar or sail as wings.
Let there be witnesses in court:
The threatening Adriatic shore,
The Cyclades,
Famed Rhodes, grim Marmora, the fierce Pontic coast
Will confirm my boast.
All these I cite.
And now my pedigree: born on Cytorus' peak,
Destined for sail,
My forbears forest kings.
There
I too once shook my green hair,
Whispered my rustling tale,

Standing from birth on that box-clad height.
In those home waters I first dipped my young oar.
Of this Mount Cytorus took note
And he will swear in evidence.
Then, whether the breeze called to starboard or port
Or kind Jupiter blew me full ahead,
With no prayers to Shore Gods for safety's sake,
Over so many lawless waves I led
My master from furthest sea to this clear lake.'
True, old lady, but all is past tense.
Rest now.
Time to begin
Your retirement. Make your vow
To patron Castor and the other Heavenly Twin.

CATULLUS, 4

## TO VIRGIL, SETTING OUT FOR GREECE

May Venus on her Cyprian throne,
    May Helen's brothers, heaven's twin lights,
Guide you, and the Father of the Winds keep all within his cave
    Save the North Wester's might,

To steer you, ship, to your goal.
    For Virgil now is yours. Remember he is a loan.
Repay your debt. Set him safe on Attic shores
    And keep half my soul.

A layer of oak, three layers of brazen mail
    Encased the breast that first dared entrust
His frail boat to the aggression of wide ocean,
    Did not take fright at driving gust

As wind fought wind in clash of will;
     Nor at the rain-prophet Hyades
Nor South Wind's tempest mood,  Adriatic despot
     With power to raise or still

The seas; stood resolute at any form
     Of Death's advance, watched with tearless eyes
The brood of swimming monsters, scorned the repute
     Of wrecking rocks and wild sea-storm.

In vain the wise god's scheme to part the lands
     With Ocean's severing bands
If we blaspheme and leap forbidden
     Waves in impious rafts.

Man endured all things by his daring.
     He rushed to oppose the gods' desire.
Prometheus with base deceit stole fire
     From its home in heaven, sharing

His booty boldly with the human race. There settled then
     The blight of barrenness and a new regiment
Of fevers; and Death's fated advent,
     Formerly distant and delayed,

Quickened its pace. Daedalus essayed
     The empty skies, though wings were not man's right.
The River of the Dead was stormed by Hercules
     And another Labour was performed.

We mortals find no hill too steep.
     In our folly we look to heaven as prize,
Nor will our crimes let sleep
     Jove's angry thundershafts.

HORACE, Odes I. 3

# TWO FAVOURITE PLACES - TIBUR AND TARENTUM

You'd travel with me to Cadiz and the Cantabrian folk,
Septimus, a race untamed to bear our yoke,
Or to that strange land of quicksands' constant change,
    Where Moorish waters boil.

May Argive Tibur be the limit of my hopes,
My old age home be its long-settled slopes,
I will ask no more when I am tired of war,
    Of sea, and travel toil.

But if the unkind Fates keep me from that dream,
I'll join the pampered sheep by sweet Tarentum's stream.
There will I seek kingdoms that were Greek
    And Sparta's royal soil.

That special plot, of all the lands I know,
Smiles for my soul; her honey is Hymettus' unyielding foe.
The olive there can with Venafrum's green compare
    And take the prize.

There spring is long, mid-winter's season mild,
The gift of Jupiter; her grape is Bacchus' favourite child
And has no need to view the Falernian breed
    With envy's eyes.

Those happy hill-tops are ours. Their call is clear.
On my warm ashes there you will shed your tear
And pay the due of death when my poet's breath
    From body flies.

HORACE, Odes 2. 6

# JOURNEY TO BRUNDISIUM (BRINDISI): TRAVEL NOTES

*(A journey of 340 miles, taking nearly a fortnight.*
*The middle part was a night trip by canal.)*

Leave the big city and spend the first night
In Aricia - inn just about all right.
Travelling companion a Greek orator, Helidorus - very bright.
Two days to Forum Apii (paunchless take only one.) Crammed
                                                    with sleazy
Boatmen and stingy innkeepers. Best to take it easy
Along the Appian Way. Here felt rather queasy.
(Water to blame. It was villainous.) Declare war
On stomach and wait while rest eat food galore.
Not amused. Whole thing a bore.
Soon night begins to cloak the earth. Stars appear,
Patterning with their light the celestial sphere.......
Peace. Suddenly there are shouts. 'Over here!
Bring her over here! Hey, that's enough. You'll sink the boat.
Talk about sardines!' Every slave boy afloat
And every boatman is having a slanging match - an antidote
To sleep. Now comes the business of collecting fares
And harnessing the mule; an hour is spent on such affairs.
Then out come the blasted mosquitoes. The boatman, who
                                        has drowned his cares
In plonk, sings of his girl back home. Frogs croak.
A passenger takes up the boatman's song. By a lucky stroke
He soon drops off and the boatman too decides to graze his moke,
Inertia soon resulting from the booze.
He ties the tow-rope to a rock and settles for a snooze.

Peace - then hideous snores. By dawn our so-called cruise

Is still stationary. In fact we haven't moved an inch.

Then some hot-tempered chap decides to lynch

The pair of them and leaps from the boat to pinch

A suitable bit of willow. Crack! We make it - just - by ten o'clock.

Wash and brush-up at Feronia's shrine. After breakfast, big shock -

There's Anxur shimmering in the heat - perched high on a rock!

We climb the three miles up like snails; but there's a consolation:

Maecenas (splendid chap) has made an assignation

With us there, and Cocceius. (They were on some legation

About Very Important Matters. They're used to settling squabbles.)

Another disaster here. In addition to the collywobbles

I now get sore eyes. Out come the bobbles

Of lint and the black ointment. M and C join us with Fonteius

Capito,

A man so polished he's Anthony's closest friend. We all go

Now to Fundi, where Lusus, the 'praetor', is full of show:

Purple-bordered toga, senator's stripe - a whole pack

Of silly 'perks' - he's really just an office hack.

Live coals too for sacrifice! Glad to see the back

Of him. Our party smilingly retreats.

Formiae next. All worn out. Capito provides the eats,

Murena the bed. Next day brings greatest of treats,

For there at Sinuessa my three best friends are waiting,

Plotius, Varius and Virgil. What celebrating!

They are the finest fellows on earth. What stimulating

Talk! Nothing can match a good friend's company.

Stayed at the Travellers Bungalow for B & B,

Just near the bridge. (Those on public business get basics free.)

Next stop Capua: today just a very short lap.

Mules shed saddle-bags early. Maecenas (energetic chap)

Off to play squash; Virgil and I take nap
Instead. Ball games not suited to indigestion and sore eyes.
Stay next night at Cocceius' villa which lies
Up above the inns at Caudium.There to tantalise
Was a mountain of food and after dinner to entertain
A battle of wit between two jesters in mock-tragic strain
Which made us laugh a lot. Then on the road again
To Beneventum, where our attentive host rushes
Around the old kitchen and while turning lean thrushes
On a spit nearly goes up in flames. Fire gushes
Right up to the roof. What a scene - panicking slave
And greedy guest run here and there and try to save
The dinner, then dowse the flames. Apulia, which gave
Me birth, now shows her familiar hills. Hot Sirocco blowing.
Crawled along. In fact, would never have kept going
If a villa en route hadn't taken us in. Place overflowing
With smoke (green wood and leaves burning in hearth). Eyes smart.
Here very silly. Issued an invitation to a tart
Who doesn't turn up. Wait till midnight. Finally start
To doze off but impossible now not to fix
Thoughts on sex. Voluptuous dreams and usual bag of tricks.
Following day take a carriage which licks
Along at a terrific pace. Cover twenty-four miles. Rest
At a little town whose name won't scan and can't be expressed
In verse to fit the metre but can be guessed
Quite easily from hints: the townsfolk make you pay
For water, the foulest on earth. But the bread is tout à fait
Délicieux. People in the know usually take away
A whole pile to eat en route; for at the next stop,
Canusium, they make their bread of grit and haven't a drop
More water. At this point Varius has to go. Swap

Tearful farewells. He's sad to leave the party. Wrecks

When we arrive in Rubi - understandable after such long treks;

Rain spoilt things - continued to vex

Us all day. Next morning better and squalls

Cease, but road worse all the way to the walls

Of Barium. The fish there! The place crawls

With them. On to Gnatia (water-nymphs feeling malicious

When it was built.) Nearly died with laughter at their superstitious

Mumbo-jumbo to show gods are propitious.

(They claim to make incense melt without fire.) The Jews

May believe this but not I. 'The affairs of men do not amuse

The gods' - or so I've learned. And if Nature does not choose

To work miracles, the gods cheerfully disengage

And don't perform such marvels on their heavenly stage.

Hurrah! Brundisium! End of long journey and end of page.

HORACE, Satires 1.5, 1-51 & 71-104

# LAKE AVERNUS
(The entrance to the Underworld)

A cave appeared, deep, awesome, with a yawning, rock-rimmed
                                                    mouth,

Guarded by a black lake and forest gloom. No bird could safely

Steer its flight above it, so foul a breath emerged

From its black jaws and rose to the vaulted sky.

For this the Greeks named it AORNOS, the Birdless Lake.

VIRGIL, Aeneid 6, 237 - 242

# THE CAVE OF SLEEP

Near the Cimmerians' land there is a cave with deep-set passages,
A hollow mountain face, the house and sanctuary of sluggish Sleep.
Here Phoebus can never enter with his rays, whether climbing the sky
Or on his noon-tide or his downward road; the ground breathes out
Vapours and murky mist and a timid, dusky light.
No wakeful cock is there to call the Dawn with crowing song
From his crested head; no watchdogs break the stillness with their bark,
No goose, still quicker to give the alarm. No creature of the wild
Nor of the fields is heard, no rustling of the branches in the wind,
No noisy wrangling from the human tongue. The only resident
Is Silence, sitting mute; but from the rocky floor deep down there comes
A stream from Lethe's source, and all along with measured murmuring,
The waters glide over the whispering pebble bed, ever inviting sleep.
Before the cavern doors a crop of luscious poppies blooms,
And countless grasses from whose juice Night extracts sleep-essence
And sprinkles it over the darkened lands, leaving her damp trail.
To stop the sound of grating hinge, in all the palace there exists
No door, no threshhold guard; but in the very centre of the cave,
Raised high, there is a couch of ebony, down-soft, all black,
Draped with a cover to match, on which the god himself reclines,

his limbs

Relaxed in langorous ease. Round him on every side lie visions of

Dreams

Resembling many shapes, thick as the ears of corn at harvest time,
Like leaves that form the woodland's robe, or sandspray on the shore.

OVID, Metamorphoses II, 592-615

# A ROWING SONG

Heave-ho! my lads, let echo's song ring back to us 'Heave-ho!'

The judge and king of this broad flood looks out in tranquil state,
He's laid the storm and quelled the waves and calmed the ocean's spate,
The levelled seas sit silent for our vessel's shifting weight.

Heave-ho! my lads, let echo's song ring back to us 'Heave-ho!'

Together now, pull oars, pull oars, and make her timbers shake,
The sky's at peace with all the world and lets the breezes take
The swelling-bellied sail, and casts its smile on Neptune's lake.

Heave-ho! my lads, let echo's song ring back to us 'Heave-ho!'

O make her bound across the seas and leap in dolphin flight
Till she groans full loud, and speed her prow with all our muscles'
                                                                might,
And let our course trail far behind a wake of foaming white.

Heave-ho! my lads, let echo's song ring back to us 'Heave-ho!'

Old Phorcus' crew may skim the seas, for us it's still 'Heave-ho!'
The oars may turn and churn the waves, but we must still 'Heave-ho!'
Heave-ho! once more and let the shore roar back to us 'Heave-ho!'

ANON

Oxford Book of Latin Verse 307

# THE GLORIES OF ITALY

But neither Persia's wealth of forest lands
Nor fairest Ganges and Hermus' gold-silted bed
Nor all Arabia, rich in scented sands,
Nor anything the furthest Orient bred
Can rival Italy's glories. She was not ploughed
By fire-breathing bulls, for Cadmus to sow
The hideous dragon's teeth; no spiky crowd
Of warriors, helmet clad, with serried show
Of spears, sprang fully-armed from Italy's roots.
Her land is not filled with crops as grim as these,
But Bacchus' Massic juice and bursting fruits;
Her offspring are happy herds and olive trees.
She breeds proud chargers, high-stepping on the plains,
White flocks, fine bulls as altar offering,
Washing them in her sacred river's rains
For them to lead the triumph march. Her spring
To birth and increase is a constant friend,
Her summer steals months that elsewhere winter claims;
Twice does she serve her fruits and twice distend
The wombs of all her beasts. The fearsome names
Of lion and rabid tiger are strangers here,
No poison plants deceive the pickers' hands,
No scaly serpent contracts in coiling sphere
Nor sweeps his length along in giant bands.
Add matchless cities, her labour's recompense,
Add towns piled sheer in hill-top artistry,
Rivers that flow past ancient battlements,
Land that is bathed both North and South by sea.
Add mighty lakes: great Como, the ocean roar
Of Garda's surging waves. Or should I praise

Her ports, that harbour where, by Caesar's law,
The seas hiss loud as Lake Lucrine's barrier stays
Their indignant waters, and the Tyrrhenian tide
Pours into Avernus with loud triumph song.
She flows with gold and in her veins reside
Silver streams and mines of copper. Strong
Are her sons - Ligurians used to hardship's blows,
Marsians, Volscian spearmen, Sabine stock,
The Decii, Marii, Camilli, the Scipios,
Sturdy in war, and you, great Caesar, who mock
The East's courage, keep it once again
From Rome's hills, triumphant on Asia's furthest shores.
Italy, great mother of fruits, great mother of men,
Fit for the Golden Age, my Muse is yours.
Of farming's ritual skills I dare to speak,
A theme of ancient honour and renown,
Tap sacred springs which until now were Greek,
Sing Hesiod's song in every Roman town.

VIRGIL, Georgics 2, 136-176

# Well known Phrases...

... and other gems

## RARA AVIS
(A rare bird)

Can you find none inside those cattle stalls
To suit your taste? Imagine one who'll bewitch
With charm and beauty, will give you sons, is rich,
With ancestral statues ranged around her halls,
Pure as the Sabines who stopped their men folk's strife
With flying tresses. Chastity's paragon -
A rare bird on this earth, a true black swan -
Yet who could endure perfection in a wife?

JUVENAL, Satire 6, 161-166

## QUIS CUSTODIET IPSOS CUSTODES?
(Who will guard the guards?)

'Lock up your wife indoors!' - But what of the guards?
Who will guard them? She knows they won't disclose
Her amours - for the right reward. She'll play her cards.
Guilt protects guilt. She'll start her games with those.

JUVENAL, Satire 6, 347-8

(MSS O 31-34)

## MENS SANA IN CORPORE SANO
(A healthy mind in a healthy body)

Riches, power, beauty, length of days,
Eloquence - these are men's fruitless prayers.
Then is there no gift to pray for? Man's malaise
Is best cured by gods. Let the choice be theirs.

They serve utility, not pleasure's creed.
They love us more; their gifts are for our good.
We kill our happiness with blinding greed
And reckless passions. We ask for parenthood
And all the blessings of the marriage bed,
But they know well what wife and sons will be.
Still, so that you may have a little shred
Of prayer, a yearned-for opportunity
To lay your piffling pig-meat on the shrine
And use prophetic sausages, ask for sound mind
Inside sound body, a heart that will not incline
To fear, will not dread death, a heart designed
To think long life the least of Nature's gifts;
To bear trouble; know no anger nor the stings
Of lust; to prefer the cruel blows and shifts
That Hercules knew to venery and kings'
Cushioned feasts. Let Virtue's path be trod.
She alone can bring serenity.
Fortune, if man were wise, you are no god.
Only our folly grants you divinity.

JUVENAL, Satire 10, 346-366

## PANEM ET CIRCENSES
(Bread and circuses)

Gone are the days we sold our votes and long since Remus' crowd
Has cast off its civic cares. That race which once had power to invest
With sovereignty, fasces, legions, all those proud
Honours, makes Bread and Circuses its only interest.

JUVENAL, Satire 10, 77-81

# TIMEO DANAOS ET DONA FERENTES
### (I fear the Greeks although they bring gifts)

The guests grew silent: all kept their gaze upon the Trojan chief.
Then from his raised banquet couch Aeneas began to speak:
'Queen Dido, you ask me to renew a grief too great to tell,
The sadness of Troy's power and kingdom shattered by the Greeks,
A night of suffering which I saw myself. I played my part.
Could any barbarous tribesman of the Greeks repeat this tale,
Or any soldier from the camp of cruel Ulysses
And not be moved to tears? And see, already dewy night
Is speeding from the sky, the message from the setting stars
Pronounces sleep.... Yet if you yearn so much to know our fate
And hear in brief the final groans of Troy, although my soul
Shrinks from the memories and has tried to escape such pain,
I will begin.

    Already so many years were slipping by. Crushed by the war,
Defeated by the fates, the Greek captains built a giant horse,
Mountain-vast (for Pallas lent her aid). They cut down trees
Of fir to weave the ribs; they claim it is an offering
To Pallas for their safe return to Greece. This rumour spreads.
They choose their men, fine warriors all, draw lots and shut them secretly
Within the dark flanks and fill with fighting troops the vast
And cavernous womb. There is close by an island, Tenedos,
Known for its legendary wealth and power while Priam's rule remained,
Now just a curving coast, a treacherous anchorage for ships.
To this the others sailed and hid on the lonely shore. We thought
That they had left, had headed for Mycenae with the wind.
And now the whole of Troy shook off the chains of ten black years.
We fling wide the gates, inspect with new delight the Doric camp,
Rush to see their now deserted haunts, the abandoned shore.
Look! The Thessalian corps was here. Here's where the fierce Achilles
Pitched his tent. There were the moorings. That was the combat site.
A number gaze in awe at the virgin goddess' doom-filled gift
And marvel at the horse's mass. Thymoetes takes the lead:
'Let it be brought inside the city walls, placed in the fort.'

Was it a trick? Or was Troy doomed and this the plan of fate?
But Capys and those who had better judgment seated in their minds
Pressed us to hurl the Greeks' staged trap and their suspected gifts
Down into the waves; cast flames beneath and let it take fire;
Or pierce the hollows of the womb and test the hiding-place.
The populace is torn. It wavers. Passions change sides.
And now a large crowd appears and at their head Laocoon,
Running in burning haste down from the summit of the citadel.
While still far off, 'Poor fools!' he called. 'What madness, citizens, is this?
Do you believe the enemy has sailed? Or do you think
That any Greek gifts are free from tricks? Has Ulysses such a name?
Enclosed and hidden in this wood are Greeks and this machine
Was built with this intent, to violate our walls,
Spy on our homes and come upon our city from above,
Or some deceit lurks there. Trojans, do not trust the horse.
Whatever it is, I fear the Greeks although they bring us gifts.'
And as he spoke, with powerful strength he hurled his mighty spear
Straight at the side and in the round belly where the timbers joined.
It stayed there, quivering, and as the shaking womb returned the sound,
The hollows boomed inside and the cavernous vault sent out a groan.
And if the ordained plan of heaven had not marked us out for doom,
He truly would have driven us to defile the Argive lair
With Trojan steel, our city would still stand and you, tall towers
Of Priam, would remain.'

VIRGIL, Aeneid 2, 1-56

# LAOCOON - THE SNAKE STATUE
## (in the Vatican Museum)

Laocoon, drawn by lot to act as Neptune's priest,
Was at the special altars, slaying a massive bull,
When look! crossing the unruffled waters from Tenedos
(I shudder as I tell) we see two snakes, a matching pair
With giant loops, reclining on the surface of the sea.
Determinedly, at equal pace, they head towards the shore,
Breasts rising with the swell; their blood-red hoods they hold
Triumphant above the waves and all their slithering length skims
Over the sea behind, curving and coiling the long, long back.
A crash of thrashing snake and spray - and already they had reached
The furrowed fields, their blazing eyes all shot with blood and fire,
And flickering tongues licking their hissing mouths. We paled, grew weak,
And scattered at the sight. Both snakes in fixed unswerving line
Make for Laocoon; and first they clutch in their embrace
The little bodies of his two young sons, enfold them round,
Devour their wretched limbs in one great bite. The father too,
Coming up to help with spear in hand, they seize and bind
In crushing coils. Twice round his waist they twine, twice round his throat
They wreathe their scaly backs, reaching above their prey with
                                        stretching necks.
The priest with his naked hands fights on to tear apart the knots.
Black poisonous spittle stains his headbands, he hurls to the skies
His tortured cries, like lowing from the sacrificial bull
That flees from the altar, shaking the ill-aimed axe from its mangled neck.
And now the twin serpents slide to the safety of Minerva's shrine

And seek the cruel goddess' hill-top sanctuary. They coil at her feet,
Hidden behind the circle of her shield. We shudder now,
A fear not known before runs writhing and twisting through all
                                              our hearts,
And men begin to say Laocoon paid a just price
For such a crime, wounding with his lance the sacred oak
And plunging his spear into its flank.

VIRGIL, Aeneid 2, 201 - 231

# DULCE ET DECORUM EST PRO PATRIA MORI
(It is sweet and proper to die for one's country)

Best let a youth learn toughness in war's sharp field,
Bear want and hardship, welcome them as a friend,
    Vex the fierce Parthian on his charger,
        Counter the tyrannous king's aggression,

Feared for his lance; live under an open sky;
Fill days with danger. Watching from enemy
    Walls, royal consort and the anxious
        Bride-to-be princess should sigh confession:

'Ah, prince and lover, stranger to warring men,
See, he's a lion - reckless to challenge him -
    Too fierce to handle - jaws a-slavering,
        Lured through the slaughter by blood's obsession.'

Oh, sweet and fine to die for one's fatherland.
Death chases too the soldier who runs away,
    Follows the timid limbs and backs of
        Youth that hates warfare, without concession.

How picture true worth? Ignorant of defeat
In base elections; keeps honour bright and clean;
    Does not pick up and put down fasces,
        Blown by the breeze of the mob's discretion.

True worth will show for those not deserving death
Ways to the heavens, endeavouring where paths are closed,
    Scorning damp earth, her untaught masses,
        Forging a route in swift-winged progression.

Then loyal silence also must have reward.
I'll share no roof, not sail the same fragile boat
    With one who broadcasts Ceres' ritual,
        Truths of her Mysteries' secret session.

Often the Sky God, slighted by man, has linked
Innocence with guilt. In spite of her limping gait,
    Rarely has Vengeance, late in starting,
        Failed to pursue and to catch Transgression.

HORACE, Odes 3, 2

# A SOP TO CERBERUS

Huge Cerberus makes this kingdom ring with his triple-throated bark,
A savage shape sprawled in the cave ahead. Seeing the snakes
Upon his neck already bristling, the Sibyl threw him to catch
A little cake of dough, sleep-laden with honey and narcotic herbs.
With ravening hunger he opened wide three sets of jaws and seized
The offered bite, then sank his giant back upon the ground
To melt in sleep, spreading his senseless bulk to fill the cave.

VIRGIL, Aeneid 6, 417 - 423

# LABOR ONNIA VICIT

(Effort conquered everything)

Man's effort triumphed over everything,
His ceaseless toil. Necessity was his spur,
And hardship. Ceres first taught him the harrowing
Of the soil, when berries grew scantier
And sacred woods denied their acorn store.
Soon too the corn crops knew their share of woes:
Ravaging mildew eats out the grainstalks' core;
In working fields the lazy thistle blows;
Burs and barren darnel spell the crops' grave,
A prickly weed forest quietly takes their place;
Amid the tilled glory the wild-oat kingdoms wave.
Farmers, unless you win the unceasing race
With nature, all is in vain. Attack with hoes,
Scare birds, prune back the shade, call rain with prayer -
Or watch while your neighbour's harvest pile still grows
And you calm your hunger with the oak trees' fare.

VIRGIL, Georgics I, 147 - 159

# Death
# and
# Philosophy

## HAIL AND FAREWELL
(A visit to his brother's grave in Bithynia)

Crossing nations and seas
I come with Sorrow's trust,
Brother to brother,
To cast dust to dust;
To bring my last gift,
Death's ritual prize,
Speak futile words -
Mute ash has no replies.
For Fate the Thief
Has taken you from me,
Your very being stolen,
Brother, so cruelly.
Meanwhile take these,
My offerings of grief,
Due to the dead
By our fathers' belief,
Gifts that are drowned
By my tears' rising swell
And bear my eternal
Hail and farewell.

CATULLUS, 101

# THE EMPEROR HADRIAN TO HIS SOUL

Gentle, roaming little soul,
Body's friend and body's guest,
Gone your welcome ways of old.
Wan and lonely, naked, cold,
You leave your shelter. Where your goal?
Where now your merriment and jest?

HADRIAN, Oxford Book of Latin Verse 287

# TO VIRGIL ON THE DEATH OF QUINTILIUS

Should suffering feel shame? Grief's show be wrong
At loss of life so dear? Melpomene, inspire
Me with Jove's gift of clear voice and lyre.
    Teach me mourning's song.

So, Quintilius, that cloying sleep is here
For ever. Transparent rectitude, integrity,
And Justice's sister, untarnished loyalty,
    When will they find his peer?

He is dead; all goodness grieves,
But Virgil, none like you. Whatever we invest
With gods is on set terms. Request
    For his return is vain. Piety retrieves

Nothing. The trees gave ear to Orpheus' airs.
What if you plucked the strings to sweeter serenade?
Would blood return to that thin shade
    Once Mercury, loath to let prayers

Unlock Death's gates, has driven him to the dark herd below
With his grim rod. Bleak balm: but pain is easier stilled
By acceptance, if divine law has willed
    That things be so.

HORACE, Odes I, 24

# NOTHING SURVIVES AFTER DEATH

Now when you see another grow aggrieved
That after death his own dear mortal flesh
Reeks rotting underground, or else is food
For flames or jaws of beasts, though he protests
Loud disbelief that lifeless fibres feel,
Yet you may know the man does not ring true -
Some secret sting of fear lurks harassing
His heart. He does not honour in my view
His firm words to the world that flow so full.
He does not uproot and cast himself from life
But makes some little piece of self survive
Although unconsciously. For when in life
A man has visions of his fate in death,
Of birds and beasts of prey tearing his flesh,
He pities this self; he cannot be quite divorced,
Cannot be parted from that prostrate corpse;
He thinks that form is his and hovers near,
Infecting it with feelings like his own.
This is why he chafes at mortality.
He does not see the truth that death is such
There is no other self alive to mourn
His own extinction, watch weeping as he lies there
Being mauled. And what of cremation too?
For if to be crushed and crunched by beasts is hard,
I find no reason why it is not grim
To be laid on fires and roast in scorching flames;
Or else to lie in suffocating state
Embalmed in honey, or stiff on icy slab,
Or buried under heavy weight of earth
For feet to trample as they walk above.

LUCRETIUS, De Rerum Natura 3, 870 - 893

## WHY LAMENT DEATH?

'Gone, gone that greeting,' people say,
'From happy household and from virtuous wife.
Gone the heart's silent joy when precious sons
Run in rivalry to snatch the first welcoming kiss.
Gone the thriving ways of youth, that bastion
Of all your folk. Poor wretch!' they say,
'Wretched, wretched your fate! One cruel day
Has robbed you of all life's many sweet rewards.'
This is a point they do not add: gone too
The longing for such joys. For if they saw
This truth within their minds, with words to match,
They soon would know release from strangling dread.
'All's well for you,' they say, 'drugged in death's sleep,
Freed for the rest of time from sorrow's pains.

But once you are ashes on the gruesome pyre,
Unquenchable our weeping, evermore
Our grief, no day will take it from our hearts.'
Then we should ask them, 'Where is the distress?
If substance returns to quiet and to sleep
Why should eternal sorrow waste men's strength?'

LUCRETIUS, De Rerum Natura 3, 894 - 911

## AENEAS AND THE SIBYL ENTER THE UNDER-WORLD FORECOURT

They trod the path, shadowy forms under the lonely night,
Passing through the gloom and the empty halls of Dis
And his lifeless kingdoms. Such is the way through woods in the
grudging light
Of a doubtful moon, when Jupiter has hidden the heaven in shadow
And black night robbed the world of colour. Before the forecourt proper
Just at the opening of the jaws of Hell, spirits of Grief
And Pain's vengeful shapes have placed their bed; here is the home
Of sallow-faced Diseases and melancholy Age, and Fear,
And virtue-sapping Hunger, and ugly Poverty, forms
Terrible to behold, and Death, and Toil. Death's sister, Sleep,
Was in their midst, and Lustful thoughts, and at the far doorway
Sat death-spawning War, next to the Furies' iron chambers,
And raving Strife, with blood-drenched ribbons entwining her
snaky hair.

VIRGIL, Aeneid 6, 268 - 281

# CHARON, FERRYMAN OF THE DEAD

From here there runs a road which leads deep down to Acheron's
waves,
Where the waters seethe with mud, sucked swirling into the
gluttonous abyss
And belching all their sand into Cocytus. A ferryman guards
These streams and waterways, the dreaded Charon's filthy form,
His chin an uncombed wilderness of white. His eyes stare fire.
A dirty cloak hangs knotted from his shoulders. He drives his craft
Himself with a pole, trims the sails himself, ferrying the bodies
In the rust-dark boat, an old man now. But old age for a god
Is always fresh and green.

VIRGIL, Aeneid 6, 295 - 304

# DEATH COMES ALIKE TO ALL ERAS

No more in earliest times than now did man
Leave the beloved light of ebbing life.
More individuals, true, might then be seized,
Providing a living meal for beasts and torn
By their teeth, fill grove and hill and wood
With shrieking, as they saw their living flesh
Interred in a living grave; and those whom flight
Had rescued, with their body now half-gnawed,
Covering their hideous sores with trembling palms,
Summoned the God of Death with awful cries
Until the cruel spasms had robbed them of life,
Lacking all help, and knowledge not yet theirs
Of what their wounds required.

Yet one day's march
Beneath the battle flags did not afford
To Death the gift of countless troops of men
Nor did the violent waters of the deep
Fling on to rocks both ships and crew alike.
Vain, fruitless, futile the sea's attempts
To whip its waters into stormy rage
And it lightly laid aside its empty threats.
Nor did the sly seduction of its calm
Lure men to shipwreck with its smiling waves
When the mariner's villainous craft lay still unseen.
In those days it was scarcity of food
That surrendered men's enfeebled limbs to Death;
Now it is wealth that drowns them in excess.
Unwittingly did men in olden times
Pour themselves draughts of poison; now with more skill
They serve their fellow men the self-same brew.

LUCRETIUS, De Rerum Natura 5, 988 - 1008

## DEATH IN BATTLE - NISUS AND EURYALUS
(They are returning from a raid on enemy lines)

On all sides was wood, matted with brambles and dark, leafy oak
And everywhere the thorny bushes roamed, crowding and cloaking
The narrow tracks, with here and there a sudden glint of path.
The forest darkness and all his heavy weight of loot
Delay Euryalus and fear tricks his footsteps
From the proper route.

But Nisus emerged and soon had slipped
The chase, had passed the spot we now call Alban Heights
(Then just the site of King Latinus' hill-top cattle stalls)
When suddenly his thoughtless heart remembered his missing friend.
He stopped, looked back and saw no trace. 'Euryalus,' he called,

'Where have I left you to find your fate? Where shall I start the search?'
He unravelled again the twisted route through all that treacherous wood,
Watched for footprints and mapped back the way through the
                                        silent undergrowth.
And now he heard horses, heard the clatter and the calls
That promise pursuit. Nor had he long to wait before
Shouting reached his ears and there he sees Euryalus
Tricked by the darkness and the treacherous ground. The whole band
Had rushed him and already he was being hurried away,
Surprised by the tumult and wasting wild efforts to escape.
What should he do? Where was the power, where the arms to allow
A daring rescue? Should he charge into the fatal midst
Of swords and hurry to glorious death along the road of wounds?
Then quickly drawing back his muscled arm and whirling his spear
He looked towards the Moon Goddess above and spoke this prayer:
'Latona's child, bright glory of the stars and guardian of groves,
Come, goddess, come with your kind aid and help my efforts now.
Remember the gifts on my behalf my father Hyrtacus
Gave to your altars, remember the many prizes from the hunt
I hung in your temple dome or fastened to your sacred roof,
And in return grant that I rout this band and guide my shafts
Swift through the speeding air.' Leaning with all his body's weight
He hurled the great spear and as it flew it cut through the shadows
                                        of night.
Offering the chance target of his back was Sulmo: there
The spear lodged and broke; the splintered wood pierced the fleshy shield
Around his heart. Round he rolled, coughing a steaming river
From his breast, and long sob-sighings shook his flanks
Till he grew cold.
                    The enemy look round on every side.
More daring now, he quickly held another weapon poised
High behind his ear. It hissed through their flustered lines
And went through Tagus' head from east to west, and stayed there
Growing warm amid the brain pulp. Violent rage seized Volscens

97

For nowhere could he see the thrower nor where to hurl himself
And all his furious fire. 'You then meanwhile will pay the price
For both,' he said, 'with your warm blood,' and drawing his sword
Lunged at Euryalus. At this wild horror forced a cry
From Nisus. He could not bear such anguish, safe in the sheltering dark.
'Here, here is all the guilt. Turn your blame on me,
Rutulians. The treachery is mine. That harmless boy
Dared nothing. What could he do? I swear this by the heavens and by
The all-knowing stars. His only fault to love his friend too well,
His friend who brought him doom.'

                          Amid the tumbling words the sword,
Wielded with terrible power, plunged through the ribs and pierced
                                  the fair breast.
Down rolled Euryalus in death and over his lovely limbs
The blood now spread. His neck drooped low and lay on its
                               shoulder frame.
So does the flower's bright head lie languishing, dying, when severed
By the plough. So does the poppy field, when bowed beneath
The weight of sudden driving rain, sink head on weary neck.
Nisus rushed straight into the warriors' midst. In all that throng
He heads for Volscens, Volscens alone, and now has time and thought
For no-one else. The enemy crowd close to left and right,
Straining to force him back. But still he presses on, to face
The Rutulian, whirling his thunderbolt sword, and thrusts it home
Hard in the hollow of his shrieking mouth and as he died
He snatched his foeman's soul. Stabbed, and stabbed again, he fell
And flung himself upon his lifeless friend and there at last
Found rest in peaceful death.

VIRGIL, Aeneid 9, 381 - 445

# THE TEACHINGS OF PYTHAGORAS

Our souls are deathless. Once they have left their old abode
They live in new homes and settle in the shelter they have found.
For in the Trojan War (how clear my memory)
I was Euphorbus. I faced Menelaus; his heavy spear
Lodged in my breast. I recognised the shield, brandished
By my own left arm, but lately in Juno's shrine
In Argos.
         All things are changing, nothing dies; our spirit
Roams to and fro from frame to frame, possesses the limbs
It fancies, passes from beast to man and man to beast
And never perishes. See how the pliant wax
Is marked by different stamps and ever changes shape,
Yet wax it always stays; so does the soul, I say,
Ever remain the same but flits into different forms.
So hear my prophetic message: let not the stomach's greed
Conquer your duty to your fellow men. Refrain
From impious killing - you may cast out a kinsman's soul.
Do not feed life on life.

OVID, Metamorphoses 15, 158 - 175

# ONE THING DIES TO PRODUCE ANOTHER

Lastly, the rainshowers die when father Ether
Has flung them into the lap of mother Earth.
But shining crops spring up, branches bloom green
On trees; these too grow big and heavy with fruit.
From these in turn comes food for our own kind

And beasts; from these we see our cities fair
And flourishing with sons, hear leafy woods
All singing the young birds' song; through these the cattle,
Taxed by their fatted state, lay down their bodies
In lush pastures and the milky flow
Streams white from swollen udders; through these
A new generation plays amid soft grass,
Gambolling on wobbly legs, their innocence
Intoxicated by the strong and heady milk.
Therefore those things which seem to perish do not so
Totally, since Nature uses one thing
To renew another and does not allow the birth
Of anything not aided by another's death.

LUCRETIUS, De Rerum Natura I 250 - 264

## DEATH COMES TO US ALL

To changing fortunes, Dellius, match the mind:
In hardship, patience; likewise let joy be fined
If good times lead it to excess,
     By remembrance of death's call,

Whether your life has spanned all misery,
Or whether, reclining in green-lawned privacy
With wine from cellar's cache, you bless
     Unbroken holiday. Tall

Pine and silver poplar love to ally
Their branches' friendly shade. Why? Why
Does the stream swerve course so studiously
     And flee in quivering spate?

So call for wines, unguents, ask slaves to bring
The lovely rose with her too brief blossoming,
While fortune and youth allow and the three
      Sisters' black threads of fate.

You will vacate those purchased woods, house, estate
Washed by the yellow Tiber. You will vacate
Them and your wealth's edifice
      Be possessed by your heir.

No matter if your stay under this world's sky
Has been as rich man of old high
Lineage, or poor and humble; you are the sacrifice
      To a Death God deaf to prayer.

We all march down his road. Inside
Fate's urn the lot of each is stored; early or late
It will be drawn - and we board the little boat
      For eternal exile's ride.

HORACE, Odes 2, 3

## IN PRAISE OF EPICURUS

When human life lay grovelling on the ground
For all to see its state, crushed by the weight
Of Superstition, who ever showed her head
In every province of the heavens, and bent
Her gruesome face to threaten mortal men,
A Greek-born man first dared raise mortal eyes
And look her square, look her square and stand
And defy. No tales of gods, no thunderbolts,
No rumbling menaces from heaven could check

His will, but rather they stirred the throbbing manhood
Of his mind to want to be the first
To smash the constricting locks of Nature's doors.
That mental force and mettle triumphed through.
He travelled far in theory and thought
Beyond the flaming ramparts of the world,
Roamed through the measureless tract and brought us back
Victorious news of Truth - what can be born
And what cannot, how each thing has its powers
Marked and defined, its boundary firmly fixed.
Now it is Superstition's turn to be kicked
And crushed, while Victory lifts us to the skies.

LUCRETIUS, De Rerum Natura 1, 62 - 79

# FREEDOM FROM PAIN

Pleasant indeed, when winds convulse the calm
Of the wide sea, to stand on the shore and watch
Another man's ordeal, not because
Someone's affliction brings delight and joy
But to behold the ills you have escaped
Yourself is pleasant. Pleasant too to see
The parade of battle on the plains below
Ready for war's clash, and have no part
In the peril. But sweetest of all to have
A citadel of peace, well-fortressed
By wise men's teaching, and watch from on high
The straggling, swerving steps of other men
Aimlessly searching for the paths of life,
Waging a war of wits, entering the fight
For rank and honour, striving night and day
With unrivalled effort to reach the pinnacles

Of wealth and power. How pitiful are men's minds,
How blind their hearts! In how much dark and danger
Life's little span is spent! Can they not see
That Nature barks and begs for only this:
That pain be parted from the body's sphere
And the mind be free from care and fear to enjoy
Sensations of delight? Therefore we see
That our bodily nature has but meagre wants ‑
Only such things as take away its pain.

LUCRETIUS, De Rerum Natura 2, 1 ‑ 21

# PEACE OF MIND

Peace is man's constant prayer, peace.
Let a black cloud but hide the moon,
The guide stars fail; the sailor, caught in the wide Aegean's gale,
Prays for release.

The Medes' bright‑quivered loins
And even war‑frenzied Thrace
Crave rest, my friend, rest ‑ a favour not possessed
With gold or purple's coin.

The wretched tumults of the mind
Are not dispelled by loot or lictor's pomp.
Man builds panelled halls: the birds of care still flutter there.
So is it designed.

The wise man's frugal table will gleam bright
With his fathers' plain pot of salt.
He will not let ambition's creed of fear and sordid greed
Disturb him: our sleep is light.

Why do we cast our javelin throw so wide?
Life is too short to waste our bravery.
Self-exiled, run to the heat of foreign sun?
Who from himself can hide?

Care shows malice: she will wreck
Quick as the stag, quick as the East wind
That drives the clouds, all peace of mind; will climb behind
Horsemen, will mount the deck

Of brass-beaked ships. The mind should not commute
Its present joys to fear of future pain.
Eat the bitter bread and let the slow smile spread.
Content has no absolute.

Achilles' fame yielded to Death's surprise;
Lasting old age shrivelled Tithonus' strength.
Fate may provide for me a gift to you denied,
One sudden hour's sweet prize.

Your clothes are of wool twice dipped in costly dye,
Your racing mare whinnies your wealth aloud;
Encompassing acres graze vast flocks, Sicilian cattle raise
Their lowing to the sky.

Does Fate have charity? For charily does she assign
Her gifts: a little farm, the subtle breath
Of the Greek Muse's song and scorn for Envy's throng -
Enough if these are mine.

HORACE, Odes 2, 16

## STOIC FORTITUDE
(Aeneas encourages his fellow Trojans after a storm)

'I call you comrades, for we have shared misfortunes in the past.
We have suffered worse trials together. God will end these too.
You have sailed close to Scylla's rabid dogs and her deep-echoing
Caves, have known too the rocks the Cyclops hurled.
Call back your courage, banish all despair and fear.
Perhaps remembering our present woes will one day bring us joy.
Whatever our fortunes, we have come through, come through the
                                        countless dangers
In our quest for Latium, where the fates point to a home
Where there is rest; there divine law declares Troy's kingdom
Will rise again. Endure. Keep yourselves safe for happier days.'
So did Aeneas speak aloud and sick with the weight of cares,
He wore a mask of hope upon his face and buried his anguish
Deep inside his heart.

VIRGIL, Aeneid 1, 198 - 209

## THE END OF THE WORLD IN THE STOIC CONFLAGRATION

Time devours everything, plucks every fruit,
Makes all move home; her greedy jaws deny
Long life. The rivers fail; the shore's pursuit
Sends seas into exile; mountains subside and high
Peaks fall. Forget our little scene: heaven's frame
Will scorch its own beauty in one sudden flare.
To die is Nature's law, not Justice's claim.
A day will come and our world not be there.

SENECA, Oxford Book of Latin Verse 232

105

## WHO INVENTED WAR?

Who the man that first gave the world the sword?
His savage spirit matched the iron blade.
Battles and bloodshed were its hideous fruits,
A shorter route to grisly death was made.
Or did he not merit blame? Was ours the sin
To turn on ourselves his gift against forest brutes?
This is the curse of gold: no wars begin
When simple beechwood goblets grace the board.

TIBULLUS 1.10, 1-8

# CIVIL WAR

Pompey and Caesar had their motives, but the seeds of war were
                                                  lurking
Among the people, those seeds which have ever plunged into ruin
Ruling races. For when Rome had subdued the world and Fortune
Cursed her with excessive wealth, when virtue fled
At prosperity's approach, when plunder and spoil snatched
From the enemy lured men to luxury, no limit
Was set on hoard of gold or fine palaces, and greed
Scorned the simple provender of past days. Males
Rushed eagerly to flaunt a style of dress scarce decent
For wives of sons to wear; poverty, fruitful mother
Of so many fine men, made them recoil, and Rome
Imported from the far corners of the earth each nation's
Cancerous ways. And next she merged her fields and spread
Their boundaries wide and lands once furrowed by Camillus'
Rough plough, that felt our ancient heroes' spades,
Stretched into vast estates tilled by foreign hands.
A people such as this took no delight in peace
And tranquillity, nor could it let war's weapons lie untouched
And be fed on liberty. So angry passions soon flared
And crime which was inspired by poverty was judged
A trivial thing. Political power was all; the sword
Was paramount. These brought the greatest glory. Might
Measured right. The result was laws framed by force,
And plebiscites, with tribunes and consuls alike confusing
The pattern of justice. The result was office seized by bribery,
The people staging an auction for its favour,
And corruption, regularly holding its annual sale
Upon the voting field, brought death to Rome.
The result was ravenous usury and high interest, eager
For the day of payment. Confidence in money
Was shattered and many made profit out of war.

                                     LUCAN, Pharsalia I, 158 - 182

# CLEOPATRA DEFEATED

Now feet are free for the beat of revelry,
Now we must drink, friends, and spread
Cushions on the gods' banquet bed
      For Salian feast.

Till now a sin to bring from ancient bin
The vintage Caecubian, while the queen
Planned fall of Capitol, wild vision seen
      Of Empire deceased.

Drunk on fortune's draught, she laughed
At bridling of her hopes, with her polluted horde
Of men unmanned by vice's foul reward.
      Barely one ship released

From Actium's fires sobered her desires,
And all her drugged dreams gave place
To honest fears as Caesar's oars gave chase
      Back to the East

Till he subdue. So does the hawk pursue
The gentle dove; so hunter after hare
On snowy Thessaly's plains, in haste to ensnare
      The dangerous beast.

She sought a nobler death, did not show
A woman's fear of sword, nor with swift fleet
Tried to win some secret shore's retreat.
      Resolve never ceased.

She turned calm stare on palace lying there,
And so that her heart could suck the black drink,
Handled the scaly snakes, scorning to blink
     As death-will increased.

She spurned the ride planned by the victor's pride
In cruel galleys; would not deign,
Though throne might end, to enrich the triumph train -
     A queen not least.

HORACE, Odes I, 37

# ROME'S DESTINY

Other races will forge the breathing bronze in subtler mould
(Or so my view), draw living faces forth from marble block,
Plead cases with greater force, mark with measuring rod
The sky's wandering courses and prophesy the risings of the stars.
You, Roman, remember to guide the nations by your rule
(This will be your great skill) and to impose the pattern of peace,
To spare the conquered and to subdue the proud.

VIRGIL, Aeneid 6, 847 - 853

## MAJOR LATIN POETS (in chronological order)

### Titus LUCRETIUS Carus c.99 - c.55 B.C.
Despite the unusual scientific nature of its theme (the Atomic Theory), his long poem De Rerum Natura contains magnificent poetic description, especially of natural events. He condemns excessive superstition and encourages his readers to think rationally about the make-up of the universe and the development of man and civilisation.
*See pages: 26, 59, 92, 93, 95, 99, 101, 102*

### Gaius Valerius CATULLUS c.84 - c.54 B.C.
He died young and was very much a 'young man's poet', branching away from heavy, old-fashioned poetry and introducing witty, lyrical poetry on a wide range of subjects. His love poetry describes the various stages of his passion for Clodia (whom he refers to as Lesbia).
*See pages: 14, 15, 22, 26, 27, 28, 29, 32, 66, 67, 90*

### Publius VERGILIUS Maro (VIRGIL) 70 - 19 B.C.
He was a great lover of nature and this inspired him to write the Eclogues (pastoral idylls) and the Georgics, which praise farming and rural life. His sympathy with all living creatures and his understanding of animal behaviour make this a remarkable work. The Aeneid, his best-known work, depicts the founding of Rome from the time when Aeneas, a Trojan prince, left Troy after its destruction by the Greeks. Roman beliefs and moral attitudes and Virgil's views on the qualities needed to build and rule a great empire are features of this long epic, which is regarded by many as one of the world's greatest poems.
*See pages: 33, 52, 53, 56, 57, 58, 59, 61, 62, 74, 77, 82, 84, 87, 88, 94, 95, 96, 105, 109*

**Quintus HORATIUS Flaccus (HORACE) 65 - 8 B.C.**
Though well-known for his Satires and Epistles, Horace is perhaps
best-known for his Odes, which combine the lilt of Greek metre
with the succinctness of the Latin tongue with a subtle dexterity
that is sometimes almost incredible. His themes range from flirt-
ing, drinking and the countryside to politics, philosophy and
death. He was a friend of Virgil.
*See pages: 19, 30, 34, 53, 54, 68, 70, 71, 86, 91, 100, 103,108*

**Albius TIBULLUS c. 60 - 19 B.C.**
Helped by his patron Messalla, he wrote poetry idealising tender
love and the peace of the countryside.
*See pages: 34, 35,106*

**Sextus PROPERTIUS c. 50 - 16 B.C.**
He wrote love poetry to 'Cynthia' in an ornate style.
Sometimes his tone is ecstatic, sometimes melancholy.
*See pages: 17, 38*

**Publius OVIDIUS Naso (OVID) 43. B.C. - 16 A.D.**
Much of his poetry takes Greek mythology as its subject, which he
presents in an attractive and often amusing style, very popular
with Roman readers during his lifetime. Perhaps even more popular were his poems on the art of love, where he gives free rein to
his skill with words and his love of nuance. Towards the end of his
life he was sent into exile by the Emperor Augustus. No-one
knows the precise reason but it is assumed he 'overstepped the
mark' in some way. His works have helped to preserve the Greek
myths for us and European authors from Chaucer onwards have
drawn from the material he provided.
*See pages: 39, 42, 47, 75, 99*

**Marcus Valerius MARTIALIS (MARTIAL) c. 40 - 104 A.D.**

He was born in Spain and came to Rome as a young man where he lived in a garret, as he had to earn his living by his pen without the help of a wealthy patron. He wrote chiefly humorous epigrams, inspired by the characters he met. He usually, though not always, chose to depict the less endearing ones - the greedy, the stingy, the hypocrites etc.

*See pages: 14, 16, 17, 18, 20, 21, 22*

**Decimus Junius JUVENALIS (JUVENAL) - born probably 60 - 70 A.D.**

He wrote satires in which he indulges in fierce invective against any aspect of Roman life which displeases him, including the behaviour of ALL women. Despite his excessive condemnation and his bitter and pessimistic view of life, his power with words and his clever irony make him a very readable author and he was much admired by later European satirists. It is revealing that a large number of 'Latin tags' which are still used in our own speech come from Juvenal's pen.

*See pages: 10, 12, 13, 80, 81*

## Also featured in this volume: